HOW TO PLAY THE SAXOPHONE

A Beginner's Guide to Learning the Basics, Reading Music, and Playing Songs with Audio Recordings

Text Copyright © Lightbulb Publishing

All rights reserved. No part of this guide may be reproduced in any form without permission in writing from the publisher except in the case of brief quotations embodied in critical articles or reviews.

Legal & Disclaimer

The information contained in this book and its contents is not designed to replace or take the place of any form of medical or professional advice; and is not meant to replace the need for independent medical, financial, legal or other professional advice or services, as may be required. The content and information in this book has been provided for educational and entertainment purposes only.

The content and information contained in this book has been compiled from sources deemed reliable, and it is accurate to the best of the Author's knowledge, information, and belief. However, the Author cannot guarantee its accuracy and validity and cannot be held liable for any errors and/or omissions. Further, changes are periodically made to this book as and when needed. Where appropriate and/or necessary, you must consult a professional (including but not limited to your doctor, attorney, financial advisor or such other professional advisor) before using any of the suggested remedies, techniques, or information in this book.

Upon using the contents and information contained in this book, you agree to hold harmless the Author from and against any damages, costs, and expenses, including any legal fees potentially resulting from the application of any of the information provided by this book. This disclaimer applies to any loss, damages or injury caused by the use and application, whether directly or indirectly, of any advice or information presented, whether for breach of contract, tort, negligence, personal injury, criminal intent, or under any other cause of action.

You agree to accept all risks of using the information presented in this book.

You agree that by continuing to read this book, where appropriate and/or necessary, you shall consult a professional (including but not limited to your doctor, attorney, or financial advisor or such other advisor as needed) before using any of the suggested remedies, techniques, or information in this book.

Table of Contents

Chapter 1: Introduction 1

Chapter 2: Anatomy and Basic Care 5

Chapter 3: Buying a Saxophone 21

Chapter 4: Understanding Music Notes & Rhythm 31

Chapter 5: How to Play Notes on the Saxophone 45

Chapter 6: Playing Your First Song 63

Chapter 7: Intermediate Saxophone Techniques 73

Chapter 8: Conclusion – Bringing it All Together 85

Throughout this book there are musical examples and audio recordings to follow along with on your journey to learn how to play the saxophone.

Whenever you see the following outline:

> **Listening Example #1:** Tuning Notes
>
> In track 1, listen to the two tuning notes on the saxophone: low G and high G. Pay special attention to the length of each note to get a feel for how long you'll want to hold each tuning note when you play for the tuner.

Please follow along with the recordings at the Sound Cloud link below or search on Sound Cloud for "How to Play the Saxophone".

https://soundcloud.com/jason_randall/sets/how_to_play_the_saxophone

Chapter 1
Introduction

Congratulations on your decision to learn how to play the saxophone! Choosing an instrument can tricky, but you have chosen to learn one of the most exciting ones. The saxophone is an incredibly unique and fun instrument to play. Its distinct sound and capabilities allow it to appear in concert bands, jazz bands, chamber ensembles, and soloistic settings worldwide. This book will teach you everything you need to know to make your first sounds, develop a solid musical foundation, and begin playing music on your saxophone.

A Brief History of the Saxophone

The saxophone was one of the most recent concert instruments to be created and was not fully developed until 1846. It was one of the final concert instruments added to the standard repertoire.

The saxophone is named after its maker, Antoine-Joseph Adolphe Sax. Adolphe's father was Belgium's chief instrument maker. Throughout his childhood, his father taught him valuable skills that would later be used to invent the saxophone. In his early 20s, Adolphe was a student of flute and clarinet at the Brussels Conservatory of Music. During his time there, he noticed that there was something missing in the balance of brass and woodwind instruments.

After experimenting with the bass clarinet, Adolphe used the same single reed concept to create another conical shaped instrument - this time made of metal. In contrast to the clarinet, his new creation had the ability to overblow the octaves without changing finger position. In 1841, he presented his first creation (a C bass saxophone) to composer Hector Berlioz, who responded with praise. Berlioz wrote an article supporting Adolphe's new design and the impact it could have on music.

After the article was published, Adolphe moved to Paris, where his new creation was displayed in the Paris Industrial Exhibition in 1844. This display, along with the debut of Hector Berlioz's Chant Sacre, helped the saxophone gain popularity. Chant Sacre prominently featured the new instrument in its score. In December of 1844, the saxophone had its orchestral debut at the Paris Conservatory with the opera "Last King of Juda" by Georges Kastner.

In 1845 Adolphe patented this instrument, along with 13 other variations ranging from the Eb contrabass saxophone to the Bb soprano saxophone. After the patent, Adolphe convinced the French military to replace the traditional horns and bassoons in their military bands with Eb and Bb saxophones.

As years passed and the original patent expired, other instrument makers began to tweak and adjust Adolphe's original design. New keys and alternate fingerings were added to his original design in order to make chromatic playing easier for the

Introduction

musician. A few notable changes were the lengthening of the bell and the addition of a fourth octave key.

After Adolphe's death, the Henri Selmer Company purchased his factory in the late 1920s, just as the jazz era was beginning. The 1920s were an exciting time for the saxophone, as it gained popularity and cultural interest through jazz music.

Until this point, saxophones looked like metal clarinets. The bent design we see today was created in the 1930s, many years after the original models circulated. In the 1940s, Sigurd Rascher created and published new methods for the altissimo register on the saxophone. These methods almost doubled the saxophone's range.

Although Adolphe's original patent was for 14 variations of the saxophone, the family now primarily consists of the five variations: soprano, alto, tenor, baritone, and bass saxophones. The tenor and alto saxophones are the most common variations, but the other three make the saxophone family one of the most versatile.

Chapter 2
Anatomy and Basic Care

Topics Covered:

- Parts of the saxophone

- How to put your saxophone together

- How sound is produced

- Tuning your saxophone

- Basic care

When you first open its case, the saxophone may look fairly easy to put together. While the majority of it is found in one large part, there are many smaller, more intricate pieces that need to fit together in order for the instrument to function. This chapter will teach you everything you need to know the first time you open your case. By the end of it you will know how to put your saxophone together – from its body to the mouthpiece, reed, and neck strap – to its tuning, basic care, and sound production.

Parts of the Saxophone

The saxophone itself is a unique shape, as it is one of the only instruments with a curved bell. All instruments in the saxophone family consist of the same basic structure, which makes them very recognizable. When you first open the case, it may look as if most of the instrument is already put together. Even though there are very few large pieces, there are quite a few small parts that work together to create the sound.

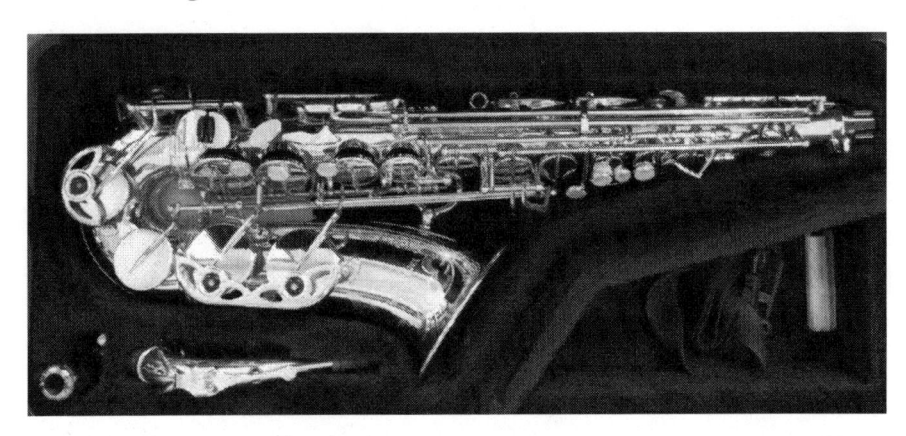

Body: The body of the saxophone is by far the largest of its parts. This is the most distinguishable part and makes up most of the instrument. This part contains nearly all the keys and holes. It has a wide, conical shape that allows sound waves to vibrate and create different pitches. The body is almost always made out of metal. Most saxophones are gold, although some may be silver or dark gray. The body contains many strategically placed holes to allow the instrument to produce all the notes in a chromatic scale. It contains keys, pads, screws, springs, and cork, all working together to create one functioning instrument.

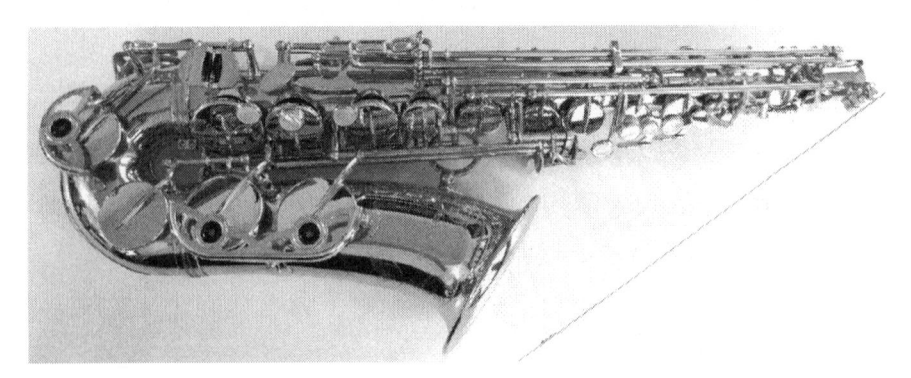

Neck (crook): The neck, also known as the crook, is a long, skinny part that matches the body in color. There is a cork at one end of the neck and a wider opening at the other. On top of the neck, you will find one key. The larger end without cork is the side that fits into the body, completing the instrument. The single hole and key found on the neck allows the instrument to play notes in a higher octave. A key, pad, metal rod, and cork can all be found on the neck.

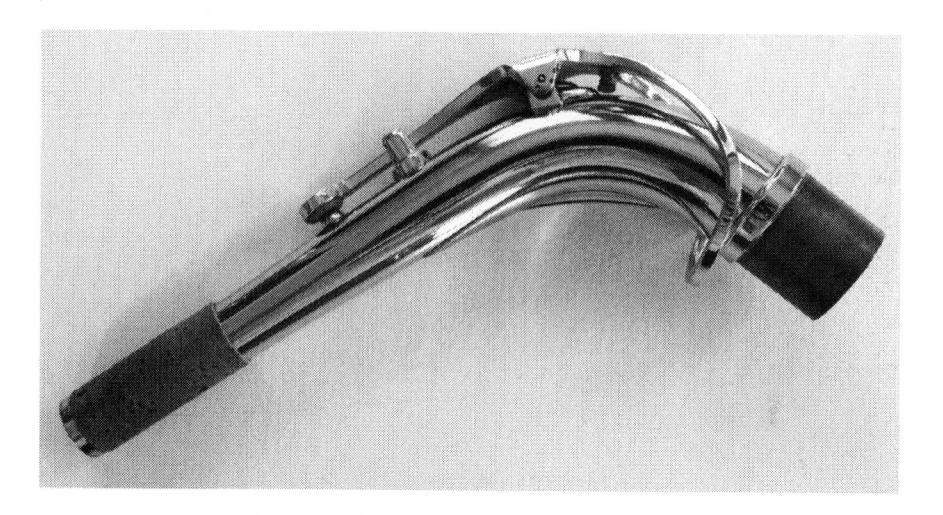

Mouthpiece: Like most wind instruments, the saxophone contains a mouthpiece. What makes this mouthpiece different from brass mouthpieces is its shape, material, and use of a reed. Most saxophone mouthpieces are made of either plastic, hard rubber, or metal and are usually black. Metal mouthpieces can sometimes be gold or silver. The circular end of the mouthpiece attaches to the top of the neck and is where the player creates vibration. A reed is placed on the flat side of the mouthpiece to cover the opening, which creates a vibration when air is blown through it correctly.

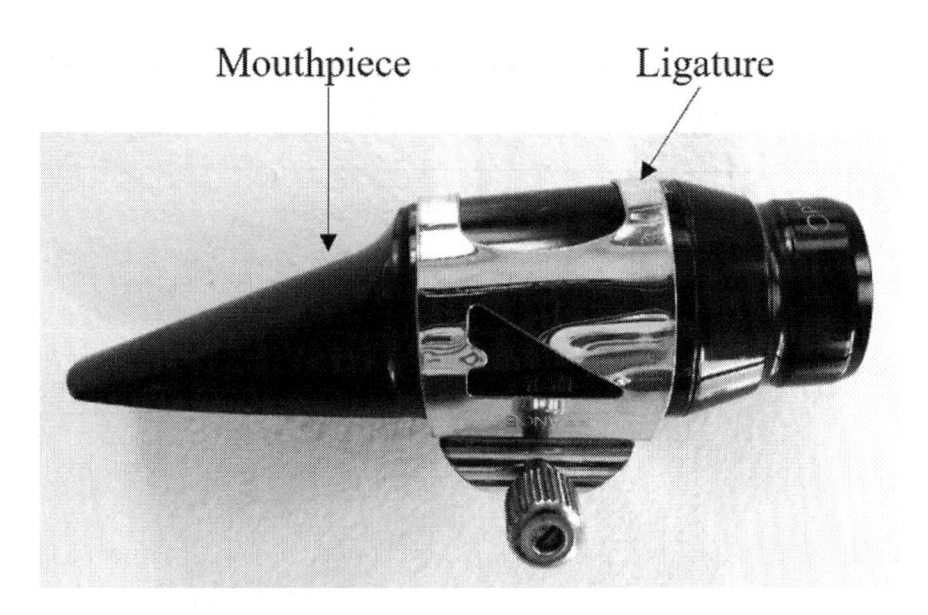

Ligature: The ligature is a small, circular piece of metal (or occasionally leather) that attaches the reed to the mouthpiece. It consists of one or two screws which allows the player to tighten or loosen it. Ligatures can be gold, silver, or black and are essential for the functioning of the mouthpiece.

Reed: The reed is a very small, skinny, finely sanded piece of wood. It is placed on the flat side of the mouthpiece, covering the opening. It is soaked with either spit or water to create more flexibility and vibrates against the mouthpiece when air is blown through it, creating sound waves. Reeds are a key part of all woodwind instruments except the flute. Clarinets also use a single reed that is similar to the saxophone's, although it is slightly smaller.

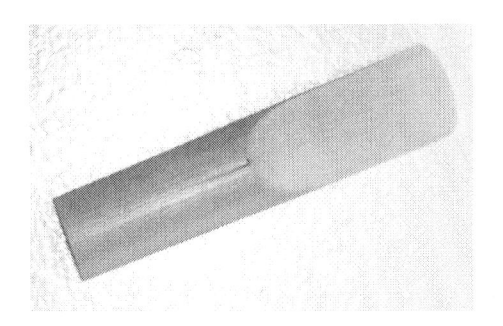

Neck Strap: The neck strap provides comfort and ease for the player. It attaches to a metal hook on the backside of the body and is placed around the player's neck to help support the instrument. The strap can be adjusted to bring the instrument closer or move it farther away. Neck straps are usually black, although they can be made in any color. Most straps contain a plastic clip at one end to attach it to the body of the instrument. Some contain padding around the neck area to create a comfortable fit for the player.

Keys: The keys are what allow a player to cover and open the holes. They are usually made of the same material as the instrument itself. Sometimes a few keys on the instrument will contain marble tops, making them stand out. Most larger keys have what look like a small, circular key on top of them, providing a specific place for the musician to put their finger.

Pads: Pads are found underneath each key on the saxophone that covers a hole. They are made with either a plastic or cardboard base and are sized to fit the key exactly. These pads are usually off-white and allow for a complete covering of the hole when the key is pushed down. They absorb sound, efficiently blocking air from escaping once the key is depressed. Pads on the saxophone will need to be replaced after multiple years of use. Once they get worn down, they turn a dingy, yellow color and appear flat and firm when pressed. When the pads are too old, they allow extra air to escape, which makes it harder for the player to create a resonant sound.

Screws: The saxophone contains a few screws, with the most notable found at the ends of the long rod holding the keys in place on the body. These screws keep the metal rod from moving, which is essential to keep the keys in their proper position.

Springs: The springs are a key component of the saxophone's functionality. Springs can be found behind most keys and look like skinny, straight wires. The springs are only a few centimeters long and are held in place by a tiny metal hook on one end. If these springs ever fall out of place or are on the wrong side of the hook, the key will not spring up when they player releases pressure on it. Springs are a common cause of key malfunction.

Cork: There is not much visible cork on the saxophone, other than the cork found at the end of the neck. However, cork can also be found behind a few keys, preventing them from hitting the metal on the body. These keys do not cover a hole, but open and close other keys.

How to Put Your Saxophone Together

To play the saxophone you will first need to assemble all of its parts. Begin by taking the body out of the case. Hold the body parallel to yours, so it is perpendicular to the ground. Next, position the body so the curved bell and most of the keys are facing away from you. The bell of the instrument should be on the bottom and the skinny opening should be on the top.

Back side (faces you)   Top

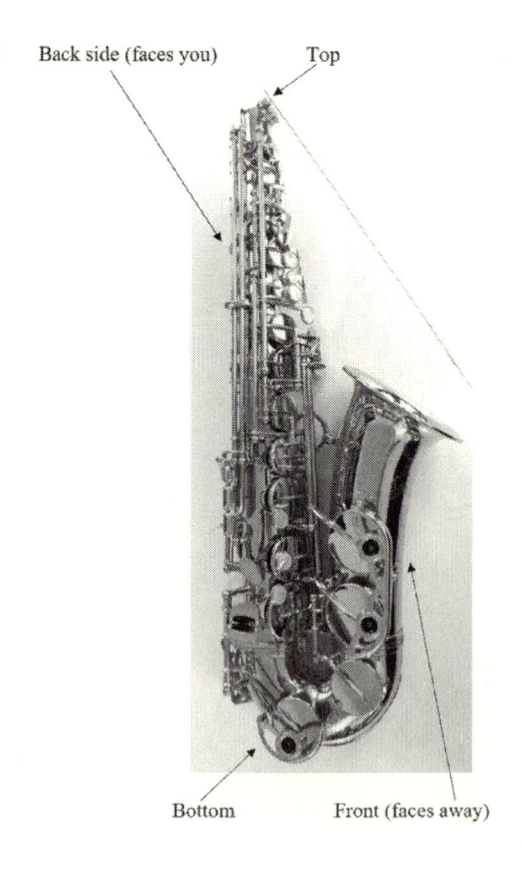

Bottom   Front (faces away)

Next, take the neck out of the case. Insert the wider side of neck (the end without cork) into the top of the body. You may need to twist the neck back and forth to ease it completely into the body.

Back of the saxophone   Front of the saxophone

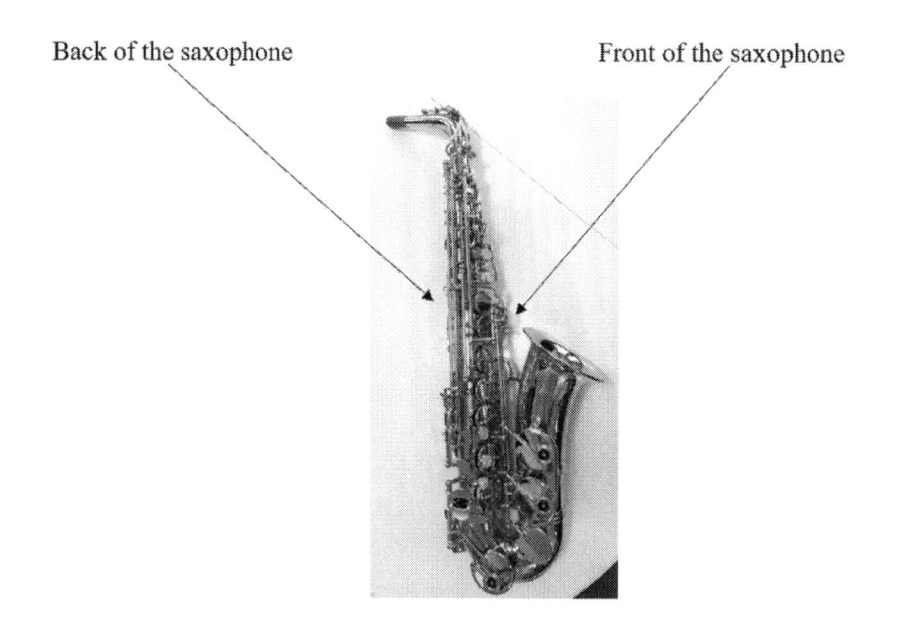

Once the neck is fully inserted into the body, you'll need to adjust its angle. The metal rod that circles the neck should be facing the back of the saxophone - the side opposite the bell. Center the middle of the circular rod on the neck with the top of the rod that sticks up from the body.

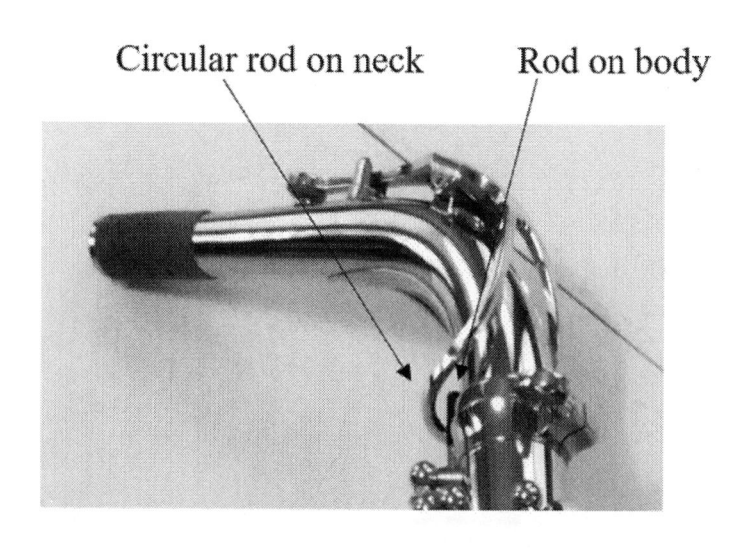

Circular rod on neck   Rod on body

After the neck and body are aligned, you'll likely want to put the neck strap on to help hold the saxophone. The neck strap attaches to a loop on the back side of the instrument. Clip the plastic clip on the neck strap onto the loop on the back of the saxophone.

Once the neck strap is securely attached, you can loop the strap around your neck to help hold the saxophone. Next, you'll want to put your mouthpiece together. You will need your reed, ligature, and mouthpiece for this step. Take your mouthpiece (without the ligature) and place the flat side of the reed against the flat side of the mouthpiece. The tip of the reed should line up exactly with the tip of the mouthpiece. Once your reed is lined up, slide the ligature over both the reed and mouthpiece and tighten the screws to secure the reed in place.

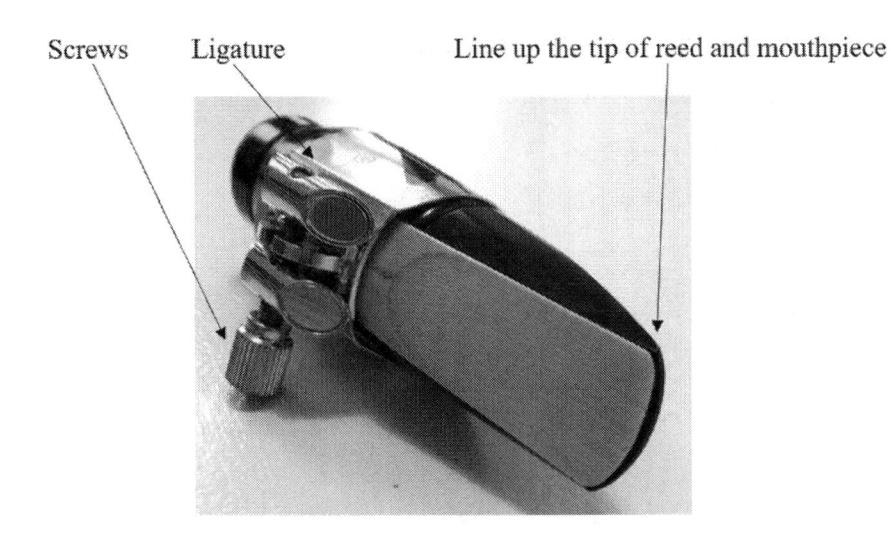

Screws   Ligature   Line up the tip of reed and mouthpiece

This is one of the most challenging steps, especially for beginners. The reed is fragile so you will need to be careful not to chip it or drop it during this process. If a reed becomes chipped or damaged, you will no longer be able to create sound with it. Be especially careful of the tip of the reed, as it is the thinnest part, therefore the most susceptible to damage.

Once your mouthpiece is put together, you are ready to attach it to the neck. The top end of the neck - the open end with the cork – will be inserted into the end of the mouthpiece. The mouthpiece does not need to go on all the way and there should be quite a bit of cork visible even after the mouthpiece is fully attached. Insert the saxophone into the mouthpiece until it stops, but don't force it any further.

Sometimes the cork is too thick and it is challenging to place the mouthpiece on the saxophone. If this is the case, you may want to add a little cork grease to the cork. Cork grease looks like chapstick and can be applied directly to the cork. This grease helps reduce friction to ease the insertion of the neck.

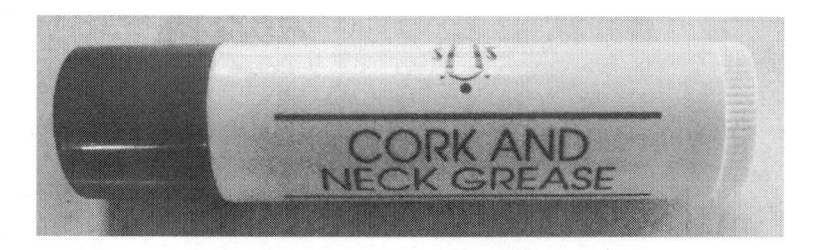

Once it's all put together, you'll want to adjust the mouthpiece so the reed and screws are facing the floor and the plastic part of the mouthpiece is facing up. You can tighten or loosen the neck strap to adjust the height of the saxophone at any point. You will want to adjust the neck strap so the mouthpiece is level with your mouth. This allows you to play the instrument comfortably, without craning your neck or lowering your chin to reach the mouthpiece.

How Sound is Produced

Musical instruments require vibration to move air and create sound waves. Singers produce sound with vibrating vocal chords, stringed instruments vibrate their strings, and brass instruments (like the trumpet) produce sound when the player vibrates their lips. The saxophone is part of a group of instruments that use a reed to create vibrations.

With reed instruments, vibrations are created using a reed with either a mouthpiece or another reed. Since the saxophone only uses one reed, the vibrations are created by vibrating the reed against the mouthpiece. A saxophone player puts the tip of the

Anatomy and Basic Care

mouthpiece in their mouth, applying pressure to the reed. As pressure is placed on the reed, it moves closer to the mouthpiece, creating a smaller gap. The player then blows air into the mouthpiece, which causes the reed to vibrate against it.

The pressure created in the mouthpiece sends vibrations through the neck and body of the saxophone. These vibrations reach different tone holes and bounce sound waves around the inside of the instrument. The sound waves vibrate with different frequencies to create different pitches.

When more holes are covered on the saxophone, the air travels farther, therefore vibrating slower. These slower vibrations create lower pitches. When fewer holes are covered, the air travels a shorter distance, therefore vibrating faster and creating higher pitches.

Tuning Your Saxophone

Instruments that are higher in pitch are often the most important to tune, as their frequencies vary the most. While saxophones are not the highest voice in a concert band setting, they are still one of the higher-pitched instruments. Since this is the case, tuning on the saxophone is very important.

Tuning your saxophone is relatively easy. You will need to either pull your mouthpiece out slightly or push it in slightly on the neck. This is why it is important to never jam your mouthpiece so far on the saxophone that you are unable to adjust it. Most saxophones are not made to be in tune with the mouthpiece pushed all the way in. Adjusting the mouthpiece is a great starting point for tuning. For most beginners, this is all you will need to do to tune your instrument. Once you become more advanced, you can fine tune your instrument by adjusting your embouchure (the shape of your mouth as you play the saxophone) by pulling the corners of your mouth out or loosening them. As you learn the saxophone, your primary focus will be tuning using mouthpiece adjustment.

When two instruments play the same concert pitch, the note they produce may differ slightly from one another. This is where tuning becomes important. Before you play your saxophone, it is important to check your intonation. You can do so with a tuner or by matching pitch with another instrument. It is recommended that you either purchase a tuner or download a tuner app on your phone (there are many free options). Tuning by ear is an advanced skill that requires a great deal of practice. The best tuning note for the saxophone is a G, which is also known as concert Bb.

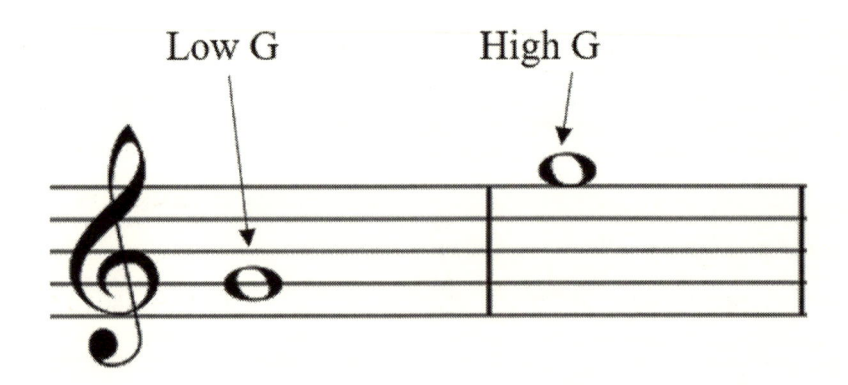

Low G   High G

Anatomy and Basic Care

When tuning your instrument, you will need to hold your tuning note out for a few counts. This will allow your ear and/or the tuner to get an accurate reference of the sound. It is best to begin tuning with the low pitch first (low G). If you are using a tuner, it will light up to let you know if the pitch you are playing is sharp, flat, or right on.

> **Listening Example #1: Tuning Notes**
>
> In track 1, listen to the two tuning notes on the saxophone: low G and high G. Pay special attention to the length of each note to get a feel for how long you'll want to hold each tuning note when you play for the tuner.

If your tuning note is slightly higher than it should be, the tuner will tell you that it is sharp. When your saxophone is sharp, you will need to pull the mouthpiece out. Remember to do this slightly, in small increments only. Gently pull the mouthpiece out of the body. Play your note again for the tuner and adjust further if necessary. You may need to make several small adjustments until your note is in tune.

If your saxophone is slightly lower in pitch than it should be, the tuner will tell you that it is flat. In this case, you will need to push the mouthpiece in slightly. This should also be done using small, gentle adjustments. Play your tuning note again after you've made an adjustment. Once your lower note is in tune, it is a good idea to double check by playing the higher note (high G).

> **Tuning the Saxophone:**
>
> Sharp = pull mouthpiece out
>
> Flat = push mouthpiece in

In general, checking one note with a tuner will improve the intonation of the entire instrument. You don't need to check every single note with the tuner when you are just beginning. As you become more advanced, you'll become more aware of specific tendencies. In general, though, tuning both low and high G will ensure that your saxophone is properly tuned.

Basic Care

The saxophone is an expensive instrument and you should care for it as carefully as you care for your most prized possessions. Your saxophone will require regular cleaning after each practice session. Luckily, this doesn't take long. Before you put your saxophone away in its case, you'll want to clean the body and mouthpiece.

Most saxophones come with a basic care kit, but if yours did not you should purchase a few items. For basic cleaning care, you will need a swab and a mouthpiece brush. The swab is simple to use. Drop the string into the body of the saxophone (it's easiest to drop it into the bell but can be done either way) and move the saxophone side to side so it gets through the curve and falls out the other side. Once you can retrieve the string from the opposite end, just pull the swab through the body. You may want to do this a few times to ensure that all the moisture is absorbed.

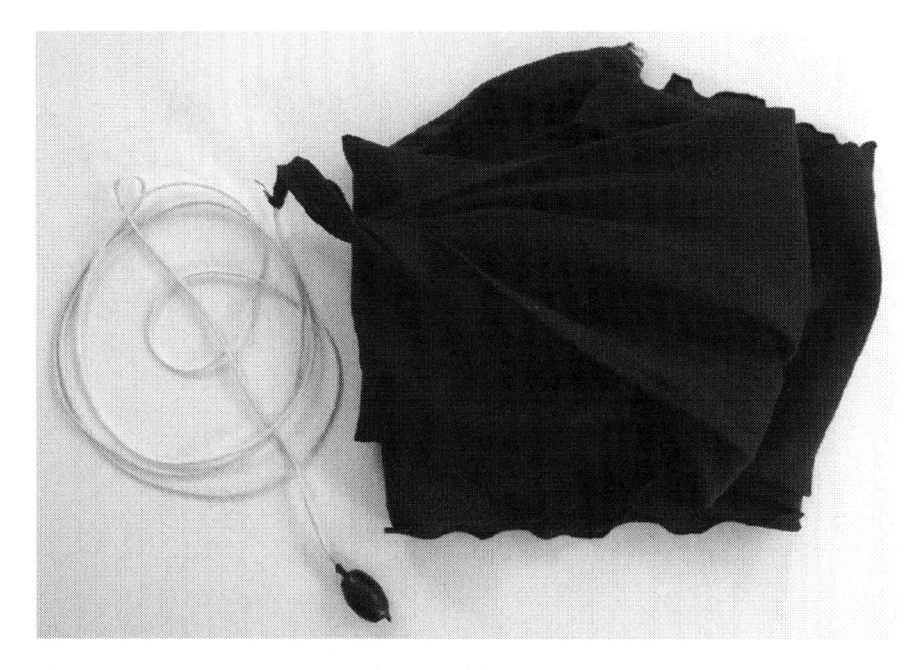

A mouthpiece brush is useful to clean away debris and gunk that gets stuck in your mouthpiece. You will want to brush out your mouthpiece every few weeks as you begin to play more often. You can also clean your mouthpiece thoroughly using dish soap, warm water, and a toothbrush. You do not need to do this after every practice session, but you should do it at least every few weeks. This will prevent bacteria from getting trapped and building up inside your mouthpiece.

Chapter 3
Buying a Saxophone

Topics Covered:

- Types of saxophones

- Saxophone features

- Popular brands

- Choosing the right saxophone for you

There are many versions of the saxophone, which add to its versatility and allow the musician a chance to perform in a variety of ensembles. Once you've made the decision to play the saxophone, you will need to select one to play. This is perhaps one of the most exciting parts of the process. There are many different features to look for and types to choose from. This chapter will tell you everything you need to know about the saxophone family, the instrument's features, and how to select the right one for you.

Types of Saxophones

When you are learning to play, you will almost always begin with an **alto saxophone**, the most common instrument in the saxophone family. The alto is most often found in concert bands, chamber ensembles, and jazz bands. It sounds in the key of Eb major, meaning that the written notes sound a different pitch when played on the saxophone. Once you become proficient on the alto saxophone, there are a few other variations you may wish to explore. These variations are also found in concert bands and jazz bands, but provide a different tone color and range.

Soprano Saxophone: The soprano saxophone is considerably smaller than the alto saxophone and its most notable visual difference is the fact that its bell is straight, missing the curve found in most other saxophones. The soprano saxophone looks similar to the clarinet and sounds in the key of Bb. It sounds higher in pitch than the alto saxophone and its tone resembles that of an oboe.

Tenor Saxophone: The tenor saxophone is the next most common variation after the alto. It looks nearly identical to the alto, except for the fact that it is larger. Its bell is curved just like the alto, but the tenor sounds lower in pitch. It sounds in the key of Bb. The tenor saxophone is a standard instrument in most concert band settings and a key component in the jazz band.

Baritone Saxophone: The baritone saxophone is even larger than the tenor. It is shaped similarly to both the alto and tenor, except for a twist found in its neck. The baritone saxophone sounds much lower in pitch than even the tenor, and usually plays a bass line along with the tubas and other low brass in a concert band setting. It sounds in the key of Eb like the alto, but its notes are much lower in pitch.

Bass Saxophone: The bass saxophone is the largest of these variations. Because of its size and expense, it is usually not seen in a concert band setting. If available, it provides an excellent addition to a jazz band. The bass saxophone sounds in the key of Bb. Its notes are much lower in pitch than any of the other saxophones due to its large size.

Saxophone Features

There are a variety of factors that affect the saxophone's tone quality, functionality, and sound creation. Most beginner level saxophones are equipped with features that make the instrument easy to play, which is an excellent place to start. However, this means that there are a few differences between student, intermediate, and advanced models. If you are an advanced player or plan to advance quickly, you may want to consider a few of these features to broaden the abilities of your instrument.

High F# Key: This extra key makes it easier to play a high F#. The note can still be played without the addition of this F# key, however it is much more challenging and sounds less in tune. Most intermediate and professional level saxophones contain a high F# key.

High G Key: Another additional key found on some saxophones is a high G key. This key makes it easier to play a high G. However, it is still possible to play this pitch without the additional key.

C# Resonance Key: One more additional key found mostly in advanced saxophones is a C# resonance key. This key improves the clarity of sound with middle C#. It is still possible to play the note without a C# resonance key, but intonation and clarity may be challenging. This key is usually not found on beginner level saxophones.

Ribbed vs. Non-Ribbed: Saxophones are made with either ribbed or non-ribbed construction. Ribbed construction refers to the knobs that protrude from the body to hold the keys in place. Most saxophones are made with ribbed construction, however some beginner level models are made with non-ribbed keys. Non-ribbed keys have no structural advantage, but they may make it easier for beginners to create a sound.

Mouthpiece: Selecting the right mouthpiece for your saxophone will have a drastic effect on your ability to play and advance on your instrument. Most beginner saxophones come with a plastic concert mouthpiece, which will suffice if you are just learning to play. However, a great way to improve the quality of your sound without purchasing an entirely new instrument is to purchase a new mouthpiece. The most common concert saxophone mouthpieces are made of plastic, ebonite, or metal. In general, the heavier the material, the darker the sound that is created.

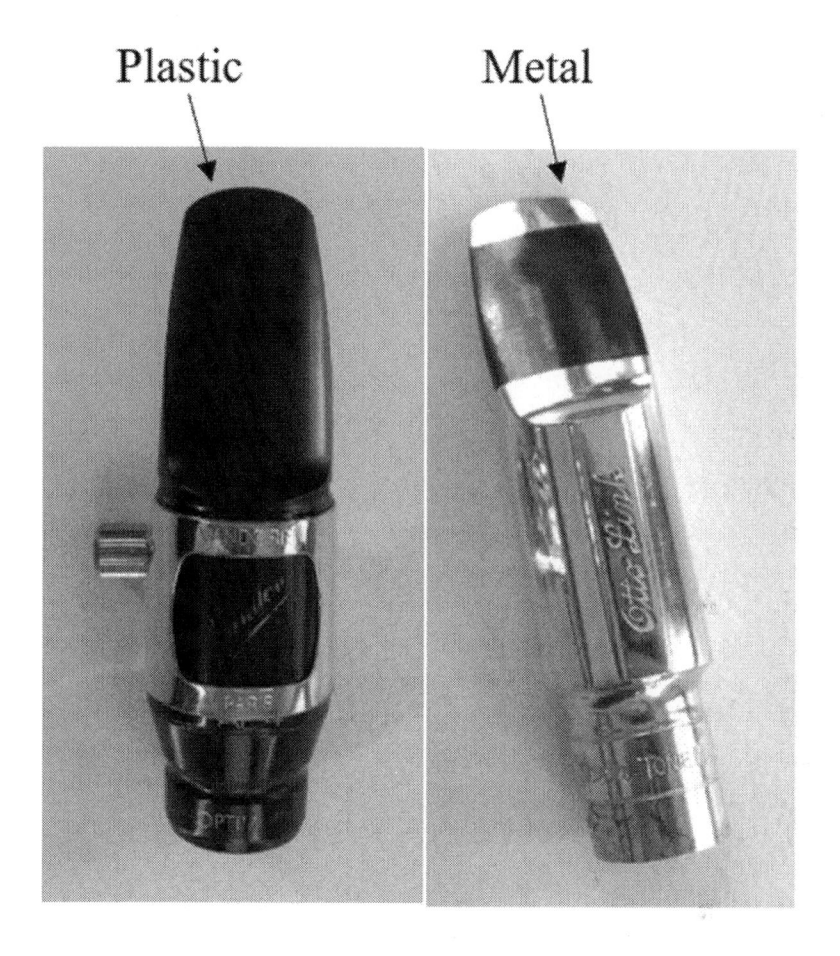

Plastic   Metal

Silver, Nickel, or Copper Plating: The difference between many beginner and advanced level saxophones is found in the materials used to make the plating on the instrument. A saxophone that contains silver, nickel, or copper plating as opposed to brass is heavier, therefore sounds with a darker, more mature tone. This is a great feature to consider when purchasing a more advanced instrument.

Adjustable Thumb: Some saxophones come with an adjustable thumb rest, which provides more comfort and flexibility for the player. It is not a necessary feature, but it allows the musician to have greater control over their thumb placement when playing.

Reeds: A special note should be made about saxophone reeds, as they are frequently overlooked. Reeds are crucial for the saxophone to function, and do not come with the instrument. You will need to purchase reeds separately and regularly once you begin to play. Reeds come in a variety of different brands and strengths. Most beginners start with a soft reed, usually a strength 2 or 2 ½. Once you begin to advance, you will likely progress to harder reeds, from a strength 3 and up. These hard reeds create a more resonant and rich tone. A couple popular brands of beginner saxophone reeds are Vandoren and Rico.

Popular Saxophone Brands

Yamaha: A Japanese company, Yamaha is one of the most well-known makers of saxophones and other wind instruments. Yamaha has a great variety of instruments, from student level to professional models. They are known for providing great quality at an affordable price.

Selmer: Selmer is a French instrument manufacturer that is well known for their saxophones. Perhaps one of the most popular saxophone designers, Selmer also provides a variety of models, ranging from student to advanced level saxophones. They are known for their key structure, warm sound, and darker design.

Yanagisawa: A Japanese company that originally manufactured trumpets and cornets, Yanagisawa is now known for their use of bronze, which makes their saxophones slightly more responsive with a warm sound.

Allora: Allora is mostly known for producing clarinets, saxophones, and French horns. They focus on intonation and reliability, making them a good choice for beginners.

Jupiter: Another well-known instrument maker in the concert band world, Jupiter creates a line of saxophones for every ability level. Their company slogan is "a world of quality goes into each musical instrument," which guides their production. This slogan seems to be true, as their intermediate and advanced level instruments continue to rank high in popularity.

Choosing the Right Saxophone for You

These companies, along with many others, provide a wide range of saxophones from which to choose. Selecting one may feel overwhelming at first, but it is worth spending some time on this decision. Ultimately, it comes down to personal preference.

Each individual has unique characteristics that make them well suited for certain types of saxophones and unsuited for others.

The biggest piece of advice to remember when selecting a saxophone is that you should play the instrument yourself before purchasing, or at least have a professional whom you trust test it out. Purchasing a saxophone online without trying it first can be risky. It is best to talk to a music or saxophone professional when narrowing down your options. Beginner level saxophones can often be purchased used. For a student who is unsure how long they plan to study the saxophone, this can be a great option. Here are a few things to consider when selecting your saxophone.

What is your price range? You can sometimes find a used, student level saxophone for as little as $200 - $500 dollars. Depending on wear and tear, these can be a great place to start. (Just make sure you play it BEFORE purchasing it!). New student saxophones usually cost less than $1,000, with prices varying depending on the model. Intermediate saxophones range anywhere from $500 - $5,000, while professional saxophones often cost anything from $3,000 upwards.

What brand of saxophones fall within your price range? As you can see, saxophone prices fluctuate dramatically depending on the make and type. Once you set a price range, you can determine what makers sell saxophones that fall within this price range. If you don't know, ask!

How long are you planning to play the saxophone? If you plan to play the saxophone for many years, a saxophone that will give you room to grow is your best bet. If you are unsure how long you will play, you may want to find a student saxophone before making a significant investment. If you plan to advance quickly, perhaps you could look at affordable intermediate models. Another great option is to purchase a student model instrument, but plan to upgrade the saxophone neck or mouthpiece as you advance.

What specific characteristics are you looking for? Do you know for sure that you want ribbed or plated keys? Use this to narrow down your search. If you want the high F# key on your first saxophone, write this down as well.

Try multiple saxophones before purchasing one. You never truly know what you like and dislike until you've had the opportunity to try a wide variety. Head to your local music store and ask to try saxophones (it's okay to try 5 or 6 at a time)! The music store representative will assist you as you narrow down your search. If you are ordering online, you can always order a few and return the ones you don't like (assuming you check the return policies ahead of time). Take your time - you will know the right saxophone when you find it.

Resources

- Woodwind Brasswind: https://www.wwbw.com/
- Guitar Center: https://www.guitarcenter.com/Saxophones.gc
- Pro Winds:

https://www.prowinds.com/category/Standard_Alto_Saxophones

Chapter 4
Understanding Music Notes & Rhythm

Topics Covered:

- Understanding the staff

- Reading note names

- Flats and sharps

- Key signatures and time signatures

- Counting basic rhythms

Now that you've selected your saxophone, the fun part is about to begin. Playing the saxophone is the most exciting part of this journey – but to get there, you first need to understand the basics. This chapter will teach you everything you need to know to read your first music book and start playing music.

Understanding the Staff

To read music, you'll need to know a few basic things about where music notes are placed. All music is read on what is called a staff. This staff consists of five lines and four spaces. Music notes fall somewhere either within these lines and spaces or above and below the staff using extra lines and spaces. Below is an example of the musical staff:

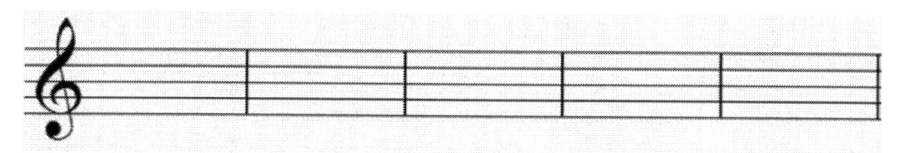

5 Lines   4 Spaces

Treble Clef   Bar Line

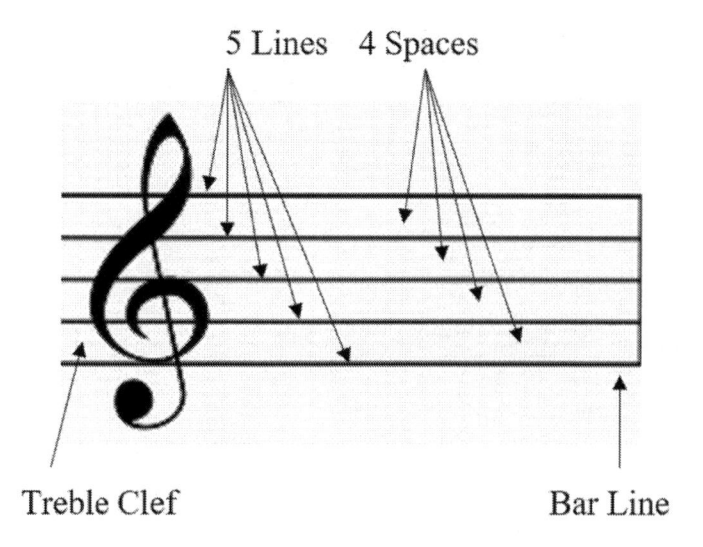

Saxophone music is written in **Treble Clef**, which is the S-shaped symbol that appears at the beginning of each line of music. The clef designates how we will identify note names. Since saxophone music is written in treble clef, that is how we are going to learn note names. A **Bar Line** appears at the end of each measure. The length of a measure is designated by the time signature (which we will learn below). The important thing to remember about these bar lines is that their purpose is to divide the music into sections - they are not a note or rhythm that needs to be played. You can simply skip over them when reading music.

Reading Note Names

The saxophone sounds in the key of Eb. This means that all of the notes you read are different than what they sound. For example, when a saxophone player sees a C written in their music, they play the note C. However, the note that sounds is actually an Eb. Luckily, this does not make a difference when

Understanding Music Notes & Rhythm

reading music, since all saxophone parts will be written in the appropriate key. However, it is important to note that when a conductor asks to play a "concert" note, you will play a different note than what they asked for. For example, when a director asks an ensemble to play concert Bb, saxophones will play a G.

Learning the note names is an important step in the beginning. Once you have mastered the note names, you will be able to look at a piece of music and know which note to play on your saxophone. The most common way to learn note names is through the use of mnemonic devices. When the notes are arranged in a certain order, you can spell a word or think of a phrase to help you remember it.

The letter names for notes in each of the four spaces on the staff, starting with the lowest space, spell the word FACE.

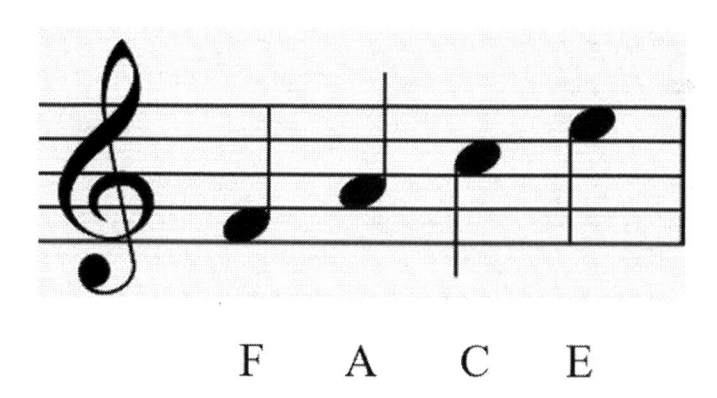

F   A   C   E

How To Play The Saxophone

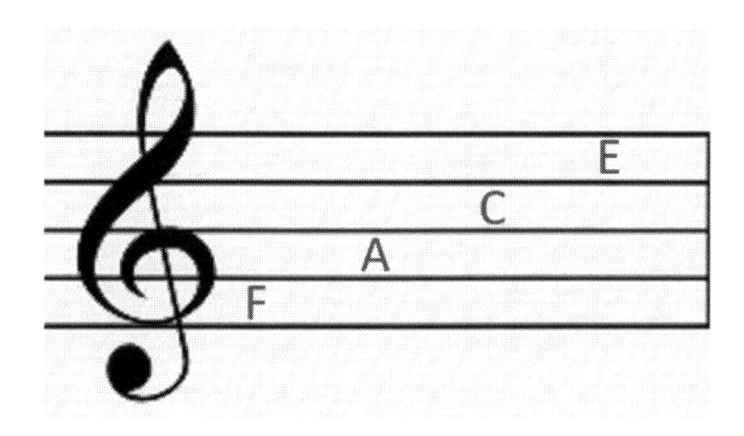

The letter names for notes on each of the five lines on the staff, starting with the lowest line, are EGBDF. Phrases are often used to remember the order of these letters, such as <u>E</u>very <u>G</u>ood <u>B</u>oy <u>D</u>eserves <u>F</u>udge or <u>E</u>very <u>G</u>ood <u>B</u>oy <u>D</u>oes <u>F</u>ine.

E_{very}   G_{ood}   B_{oy}   D_{eserves}   F_{udge}

Understanding Music Notes & Rhythm

Flats and Sharps

Flats and sharps, otherwise known as accidentals, are symbols that appear next to a note to either lower or raise its pitch one half step. When you see a flat or sharp next to a note, be aware that it is played with a different fingering on your saxophone. For example, a regular B has one fingering, whereas a B flat has another. A flat sign looks like a lowercase B: b, and a sharp sign looks like the number symbol: #. In a band setting, saxophones typically find themselves playing sharps.

To write out the letter names of a note that is flat (B flat, for example) you write the symbol after the letter: Bb. To write out F sharp, you would write F#. However, in the music, the flats and sharps always appear directly in front of the note.

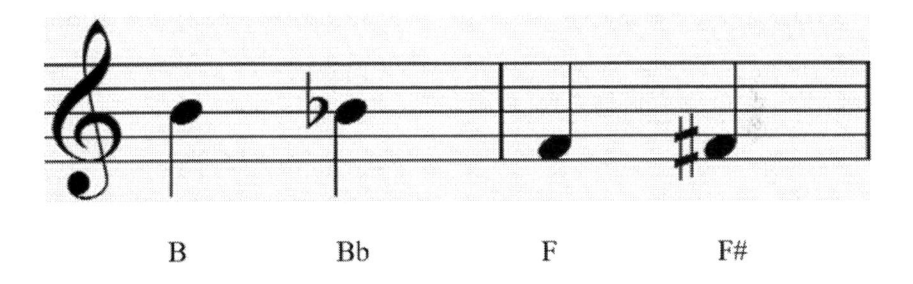

B   Bb   F   F#

Key Signatures and Time Signatures

Another place flats and sharps can be found is in what's called the **key signature**. At the beginning of a piece of music, flats and sharps often appear immediately after the treble clef. These accidentals appear either in a space or on a line and designate that note to be flat/sharp throughout the entire song. For example:

How To Play The Saxophone

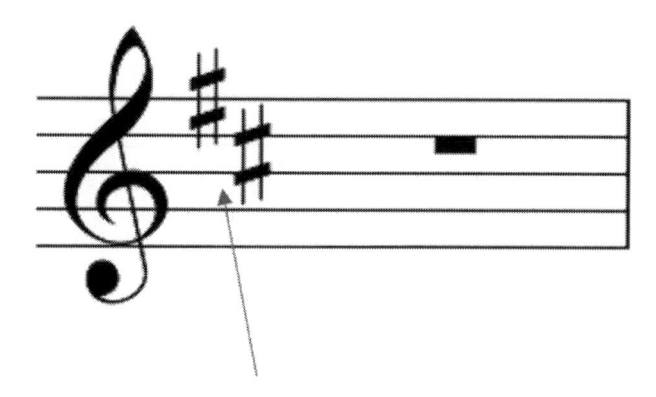

This key signature contains two sharps. To determine the notes that are sharp, you will need to use EGBDF (Every Good Boy Deserves Fudge) if the sharp is on a line, and FACE if the sharp is in a space.

The first sharp in this key signature appears on a line – the top line, or fifth line from the bottom. Using the saying "every good boy deserves fudge," we can determine that the fifth letter (Fudge) is an F. Therefore, all of the F's we see in this song will be sharp: F#.

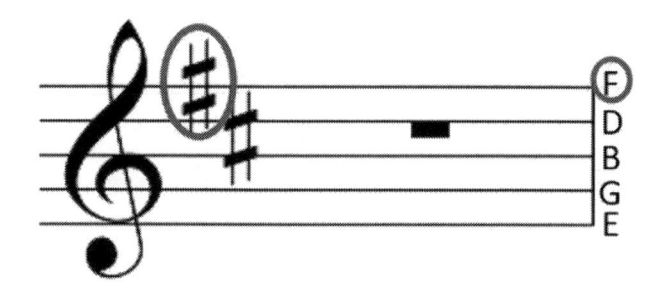

The second sharp in this key signature appears in a space – the third space from the bottom. Using the word FACE, we can determine that the third space is the letter C. Therefore, all C's we see in this song will also be sharp: C#.

Understanding Music Notes & Rhythm

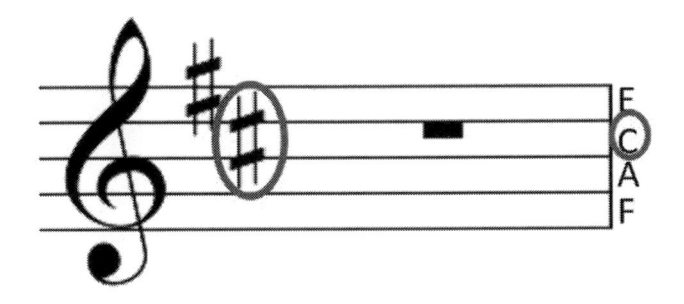

The key signature will vary greatly once you begin to read more challenging music, but a common key signature in beginner saxophone music is one containing no flats or sharps, and one containing one sharp – F#.

Another notation you will see at the beginning of a piece of music is the **time signature**. As mentioned before, the time signature determines how many beats fall into each measure and what type of note gets a beat. The time signature looks like a fraction, with one number above another, and appears directly after the key signature in a piece of music. It will look something like this:

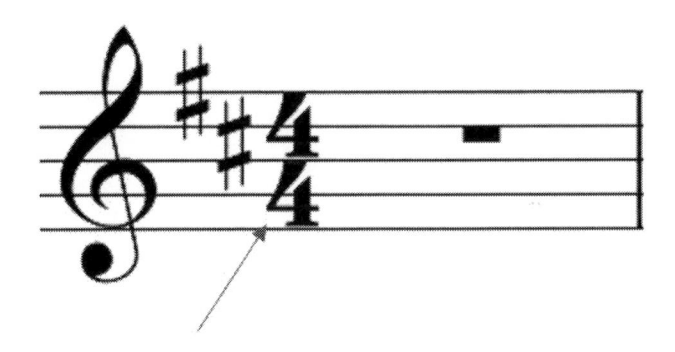

This time signature is called 4/4 (read: four four), otherwise known as common time. The top number tells us how many notes are in a measure (in this case, four notes) and the bottom number tells us what note gets the beat. To figure out what type of note gets the beat, replace the top number with a one and read the time signature as if it were a fraction. For example, ¼ is a quarter. This means the quarter note gets the beat. Now we know that a quarter note will receive one beat, and four quarter notes make up a measure. At the end of every measure you will find a bar line.

This is the most common key signature (4/4) you will find - hence its name, common time - especially in beginner saxophone music. Now that we understand the basic symbols and letter names, it's time to put them into action with some rhythm.

Counting Basic Rhythms

The most basic skill you will utilize to understand rhythm is keeping a steady beat. When you listen to a piece of music and find yourself tapping your toe, clapping along, or swaying to the music, you are moving to the beat of the music. The ability to "feel" a piece of music means that you can identify the pulse of the music. We use this sense of pulse when counting any type of rhythm – from basic to advanced.

This section will discuss the basic rhythms you will find in saxophone music. Understanding these rhythms will allow you to play a wide variety of music. They are found in every type of music – no matter its difficulty, style, or instrumentation. These rhythms provide the foundation you will use throughout the rest

Understanding Music Notes & Rhythm

of your musical career. Let's look at some basic music notes and rests. The four types of note rhythms we will learn are as follows:

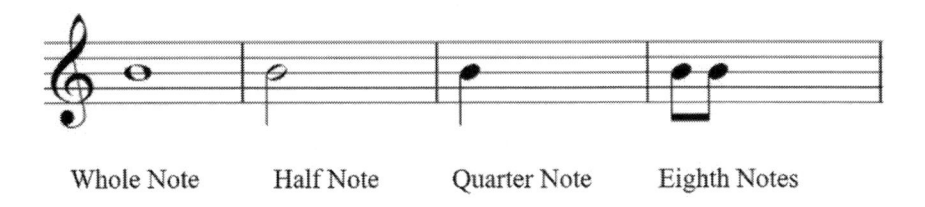

Whole Note   Half Note   Quarter Note   Eighth Notes

When reading rhythms, we begin by learning to count each beat using a number. Each beat receives one number and we continue counting until we reach the end of the measure (shown by a bar line). For example, in common time, the top number of the key signature is four. This means that there are four beats (counts) in each measure. We will count 1-2-3-4, and then start over once we reach 4: 1-2-3-4, 1-2-3-4, etc. In this time signature, a quarter note receives the beat, which means that a **quarter note receives one count**.

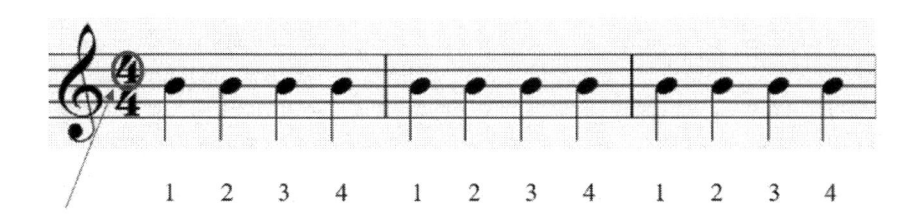

This number tells us that there are four beats in a measure, meaning we count to four and then start over.

A **half note receives two beats**, or two counts. A half note is identified by an open note (not colored black) with a stem.

How To Play The Saxophone

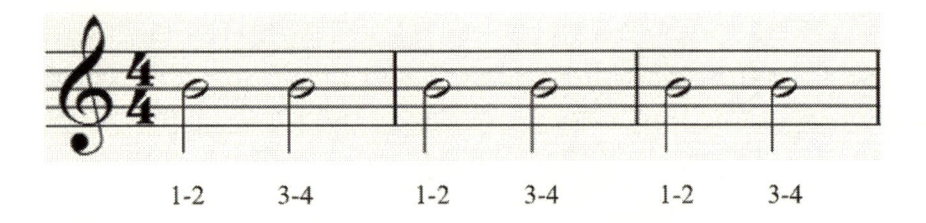

```
1-2   3-4    1-2   3-4    1-2   3-4
```

A **whole note receives four beats**, or four counts. A whole note is identified by an open note with no stem. A whole note looks like an oval on the staff.

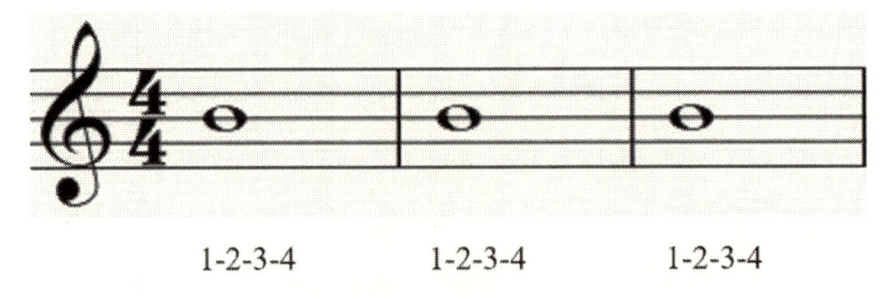

```
1-2-3-4        1-2-3-4        1-2-3-4
```

These three basic rhythms make up most beginner saxophone songs. Once you get into intermediate music, you may find some eighth notes in your songs. Eighth notes are unlike quarter notes, half notes, and whole notes because **one eighth note receives only half a beat**. This means that two eighth notes fit into one beat; they are played twice as fast as a quarter note.

When counting eighth notes, the first one always receives the beat (or the number). The second eighth note is counted by saying "and" (&). A full measure of eighth notes would be counted 1-&-2-&-3-&-4-&. Eighth notes look like quarter notes as they are colored in black and have a stem. The difference is that an eighth note has a flag attached to its stem.

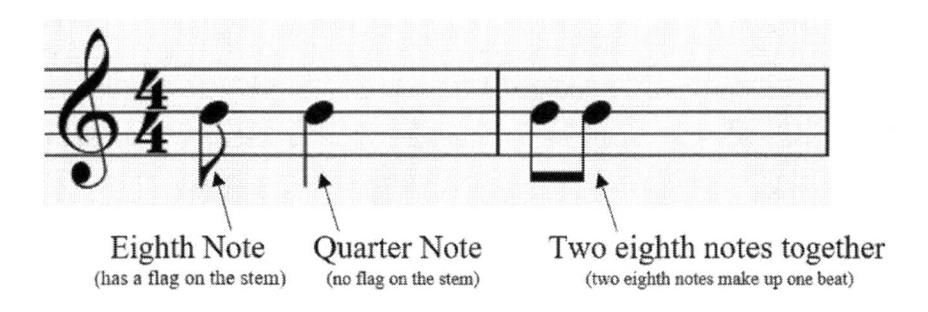

Understanding Music Notes & Rhythm

Eighth Note
(has a flag on the stem)

Quarter Note
(no flag on the stem)

Two eighth notes together
(two eighth notes make up one beat)

When taking up a full measure, eighth notes would be counted as follows:

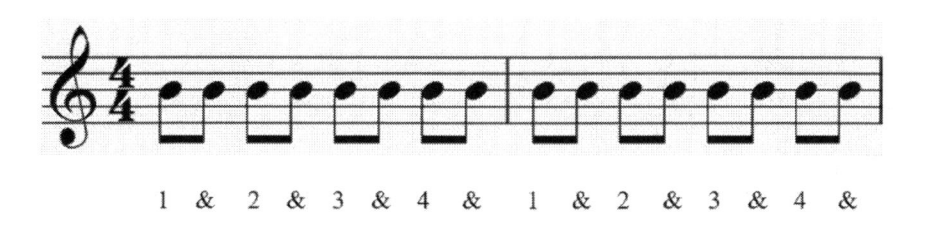

1 & 2 & 3 & 4 &   1 & 2 & 3 & 4 &

Whole Note = 4 Beats

Half Note = 2 Beats

Quarter Note = 1 Beat

Eighth Note = ½ Beat

Similarly, there are also rests in music that correspond to each of these notes. A **rest** means that there is silence; no sound or music is played during a rest. We will discuss three basic types of rests in this chapter: a whole rest, half rest, and quarter rest.

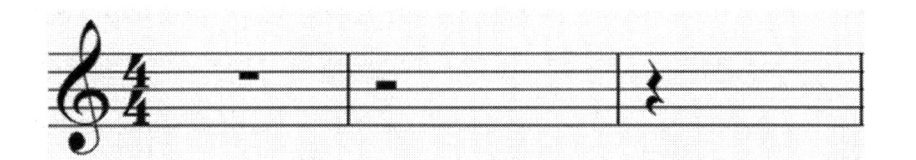

Whole Rest   Half Rest   Quarter Rest

Each of these rests receives the same number of beats as the corresponding note. For example, a **whole** rest receives four beats, just as a **whole** note receives four beats.

> Whole Rest = 4 Beats
>
> Half Rest = 2 Beats
>
> Quarter Rest = 1 Beat

You may notice that the whole rest and half rest look similar. The difference between the whole and half rest lies in the position in which they are found on the staff. A whole rest hangs below the line, whereas a half rests sits above the line. A common way to remember this is that a whole rest is "in the hole," while a half rest "looks like a hat." Rests are counted numerically, just as the notes were counted above.

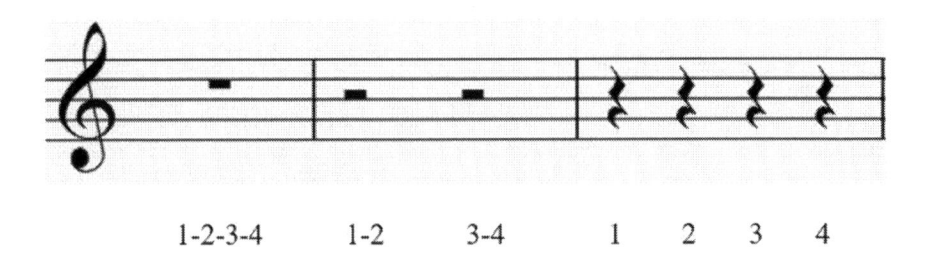

1-2-3-4   1-2   3-4   1   2   3   4

There are also eighth rests, which receive half of a beat, but we will not get into those in this chapter. Eighth rests are not usually found in beginner saxophone music, as they are more of an intermediate technique.

While learning basic rhythm counting for the first time may feel overwhelming, it makes more sense when put into context. Once you begin reading music and playing your first songs, these rhythms will start to feel familiar. After a little bit of practice, you will be counting many different rhythms without even stopping to think about it.

Chapter 5

How to Play Notes on the Saxophone

Topics Covered:

- Proper posture and breathing

- Saxophone embouchure

- How to hold the saxophone

- Notes and fingerings on the saxophone

- Tonguing and articulation

Now that you have a basic understanding of note names and rhythms, you are ready to begin playing! All the music theory that you just learned will now come into play as you begin playing different notes. This chapter will teach you what you need to know to breathe properly, make sound with your saxophone, and play different notes.

Proper Posture and Breathing

Playing any wind instrument requires a great deal of air and breath support. To do this, you'll need to make sure you are playing with proper posture. If your upper body is hunched over, your lungs and diaphragm will not be able to fully expand, thus limiting your air supply and diminishing the quality of your sound.

To avoid this, it's best to learn proper posture before you even begin playing. You can choose to either sit or stand. If you choose to stand, your upper body is prevented from slouching as dramatically as when you are sitting, thus eliminating most of the poor posture issues you may encounter in a chair. If you choose to play while sitting, you will need to be especially aware of your posture.

You should begin by sitting on the very front edge of your chair, with your back away from the back of the chair. Plant your feet firmly on the floor in front of you. Sit up tall, so your back is fully straightened. A good way to test this is to stand up once you have positioned your feet, and then sit back down. Your upper body should remain in the exact same position when you sit back down as it was when you were standing. Keep your shoulders back, allowing plenty of room for your chest and diaphragm to expand.

How to Play Notes on the Saxophone

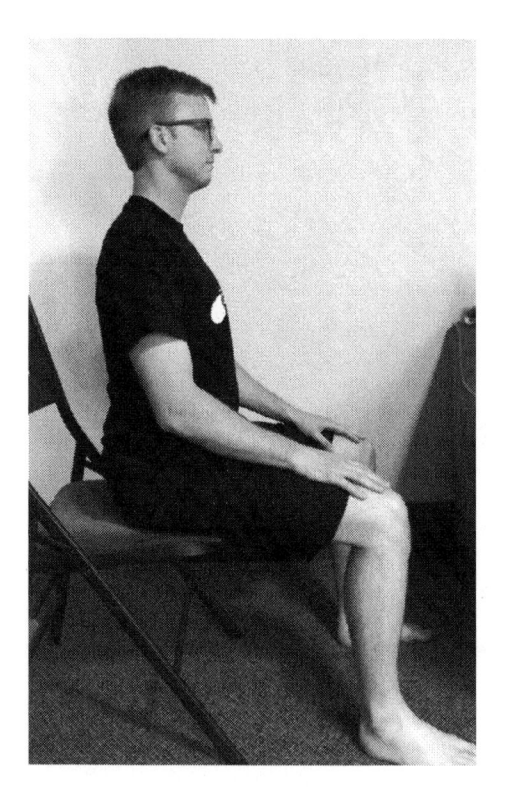

Contrary to our intuition, deep breathing is achieved by expanding the diaphragm, not the lungs. When you inhale deeply, focus on expanding your diaphragm, which is located beneath your ribs, right around your stomach. Your shoulders should never rise when you take a deep breath. Take a deep breath and practice expanding your stomach as far as you can. Practice breathing in slowly, until your diaphragm is completely full.

A great breathing exercise is to practice breathing in and out at different speeds. To practice this, begin by inhaling for four counts and exhaling for four counts. Immediately after exhaling, inhale for six counts and then exhale for six counts. Next, inhale for eight and exhale for eight. Then inhale for ten and exhale for ten. Finally, inhale for twelve and exhale for twelve.

> **Breathing Exercise**
>
> - 4 count inhale, 4 count exhale
> - 6 count inhale, 6 count exhale
> - 8 count inhale, 8 count exhale
> - 10 count inhale, 10 count exhale
> - 12 count inhale, 12 count exhale

This exercise should be completed with no breaks in between, so you are continuously inhaling or exhaling. The goal of the exercise is to completely fill your diaphragm with air by the end of your inhale. You will need to take in air faster when you only have four counts, and much slower when you inhale for twelve. You will have the same goal on the exhale – you should completely empty your air by the end of the exhalation period.

This is not the most exciting exercise, but it will pay off big time when you play your saxophone. Having solid fundamentals in place will allow you to progress much quicker.

Saxophone Embouchure

Once your posture is in place and you have practiced a few breathing exercises, you are ready to make your first sounds on the saxophone. Making a proper sound involves much more than just blowing air through the mouthpiece. To begin, you will want to assemble your reed and mouthpiece to practice creating the proper embouchure before attaching the full instrument.

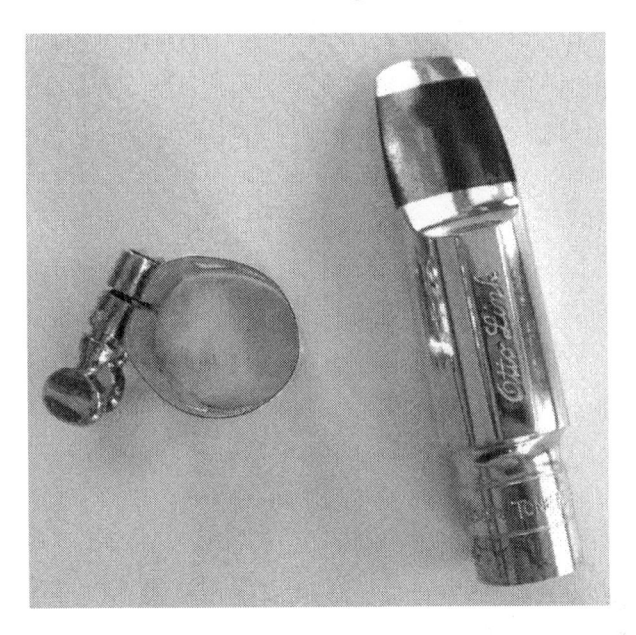

To assemble your mouthpiece, you will first need to take the mouthpiece cap and ligature off. Take your reed out of its case and place the flat side of the reed against the flat side of the mouthpiece. Line the tip of the reed up with the tip of the mouthpiece and carefully slide your ligature overtop, so the screws are on the side with the reed. Be especially careful not to accidentally hit the reed, as this could damage it. Once the ligature is over the reed and mouthpiece, tighten the screws.

How To Play The Saxophone

Tip of the reed lines up with the tip of the mouthpiece

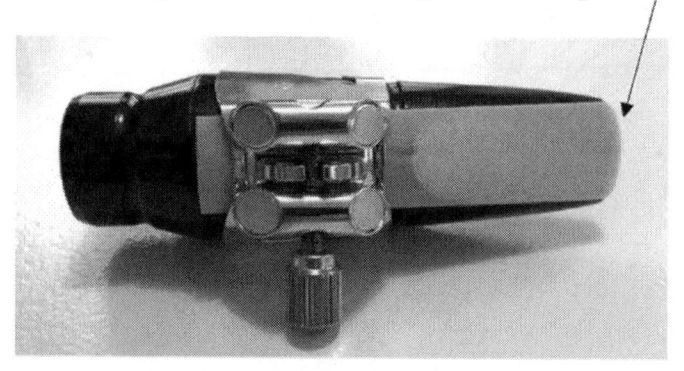

Once your mouthpiece is assembled, you are ready to practice making sounds on it. Before you put any part of your saxophone together, you will want to get a feel for the correct embouchure using just your mouthpiece.

To begin, you will bring your mouthpiece up to your mouth with the reed on the bottom and plastic on top. Hold the mouthpiece with just your fingers, being careful not to cover the opening or press on the reed. Place your top front teeth on the top of the mouthpiece. Your teeth should rest on the mouthpiece near the edge, just slightly away from the tip.

How to Play Notes on the Saxophone

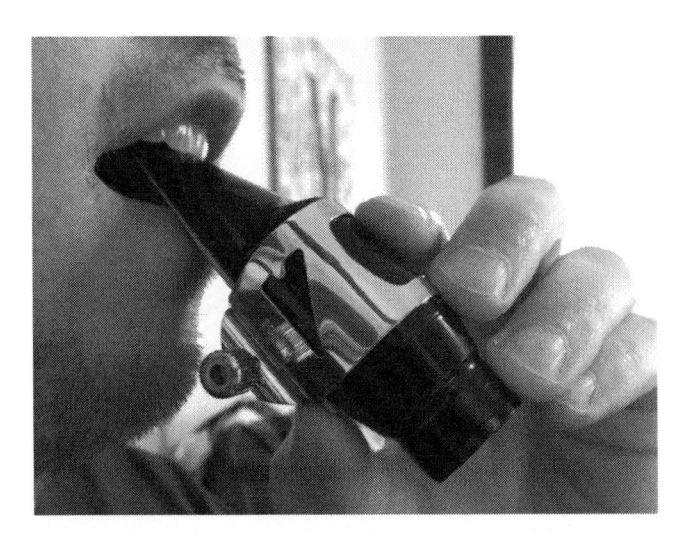

To complete the embouchure, you will want to cover your lower teeth with your lower lip. Only your top teeth should touch the mouthpiece. Close your mouth, placing pressure on the reed with your lower lip. Tighten the corners of your mouth by pulling them back and making sure the sides of your cheeks are flat (be careful not to puff your cheeks). Using the same breath support as you did in the breathing exercises, exhale into the mouthpiece while placing slight pressure on the reed.

You will need to use a steady air stream to create enough resistance to make a sound. Simply exhaling will not be enough. Using your abdomen, strongly exhale, keeping the air moving for more than just a few counts (much like you did during the breathing exercise). It may take a bit of experimentation to find the set up that works for you, but once you create your first sound you will no doubt be able to recreate it much quicker.

> **Listening Example #2: Making a Sound on the Mouthpiece**
>
> When you practice playing just the mouthpiece, the sound may surprise you. Notice how the sound produced by just the mouthpiece is quite different than the sound of a full saxophone.

How to Hold the Saxophone

Once you feel comfortable making a sound on the mouthpiece, you are ready to attach the neck and body. Put your saxophone together as discussed in the beginning chapters of this book. Make sure to align your mouthpiece so that the reed is facing down and the plastic is facing up, and center the curved rod on the neck around the metal rod at the top of the body.

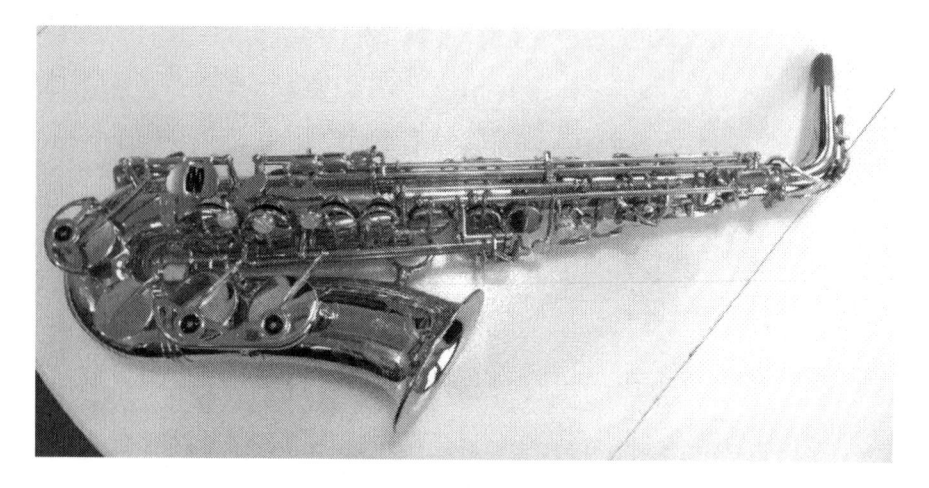

Once you have your saxophone and mouthpiece together, you will want to attach the neck strap. Place the looped end of the neck strap around your neck, and attach the clasp to the hook on the back of the saxophone.

How to Play Notes on the Saxophone

Once the saxophone is securely attached, you will want to adjust the neck strap so that the mouthpiece falls comfortably at the level of your mouth. This may involve tightening or loosening the neck strap. When holding the saxophone next to your body, you have two options: you can either hold the saxophone between your legs or to the right side of your legs. Most players hold their instrument off to the side, but the decision is ultimately up to you depending on which position feels most comfortable.

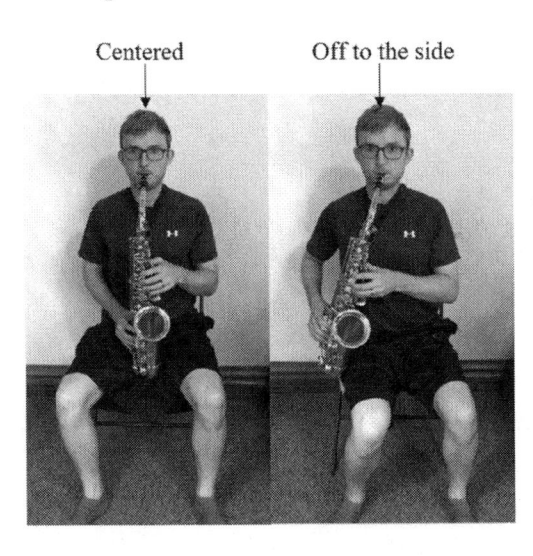

Centered | Off to the side

Once your neck strap is adjusted and you have decided where to hold your saxophone, you will now want to get your finger position set up. Both hands will reach around the saxophone to press the keys from the front. Your right hand is used to reach the bottom keys and your left hand reaches the top keys.

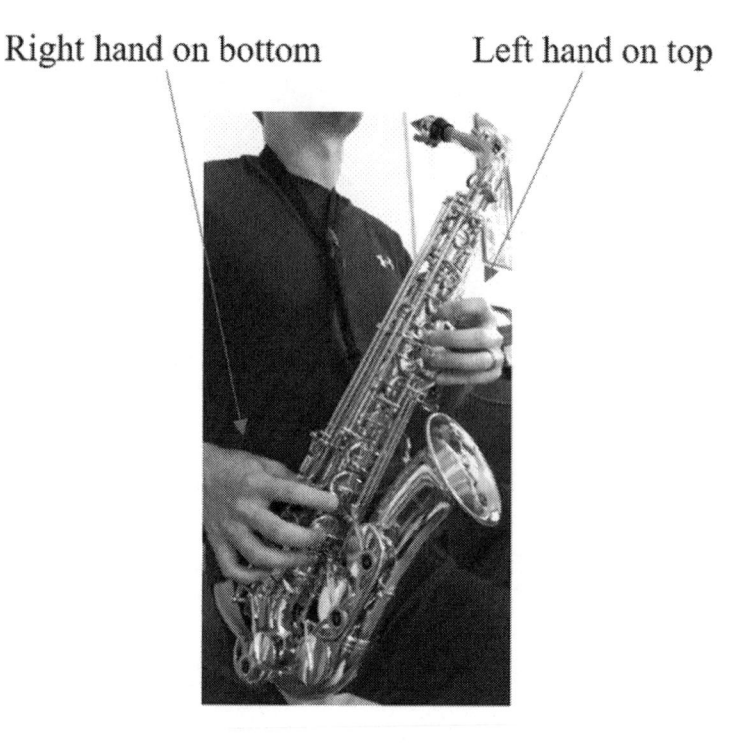

Right hand on bottom   **Left hand on top**

First, we'll set up your right hand. Your right pointer, middle, and ring fingers will reach around the saxophone to rest on the bottom three circular keys. Make sure to rest your fingers on the small circle keys (they are usually white), not the large circle keys underneath. Your right pinky will rest on the top side key near the bottom of the instrument.

How to Play Notes on the Saxophone

Your right thumb can rest against the thumb rest on the back of the saxophone, near the bottom of the instrument. Adjust your thumb so it is resting in a comfortable position to help support the saxophone, without putting pressure on the top of the thumb rest.

Thumb rest

Next, take your left hand and reach your fingers around the saxophone to access the keys on the front. Your left index, middle, and right fingers will rest on the top three keys – skipping a key between your index and middle finger. Again, make sure your fingers are resting on the small circles on top of the keys, not the big circular keys themselves. Your left pinky will rest on the top side key, which is shaped like more of an oval than a circle.

Skip a key between pointer and middle finger

How to Play Notes on the Saxophone

Place your thumb on the circular thumb rest on the back of the saxophone, just below the oval shaped octave key.

Once your fingers are in their proper position, you may need to readjust your neck strap to get the instrument at a comfortable height. Your fingers should reach the keys and saxophone with ease, so you should not have to crane your neck up or down to reach the mouthpiece. It may take a bit of experimentation to get the neck strap adjusted properly, but it will be worth the time to find a comfortable playing position.

Notes and Fingerings on the Saxophone

The saxophone has the ability to play every note in a chromatic scale. As mentioned before, a regular F has a different fingering than an F#. We are going to learn the finger positions for the notes in a G scale, which is a concert key of Bb. Bb is the most common key for beginner band music, which means that a G major scale is the most common key signature in beginner saxophone music. This scale covers a wide range of notes, but even so, once you get more advanced you may wish to play music that involves notes that are outside of this scale. When you get to this point, you can find many saxophone fingering charts for free online or in the back of your music book. A great thing about the saxophone is that most notes with the same name (for example, low **G** and high **G**) are fingered the same way, even if they are in different octaves.

We are first going to learn the notes in a G major scale. The G major scale looks like this:

G A B C D E F# G

It may look slightly different if there is a key signature. This key signature tells us that F is sharp, so we don't need to see the sharp sign next to this note. The scale below consists of the same notes and finger positions as above.

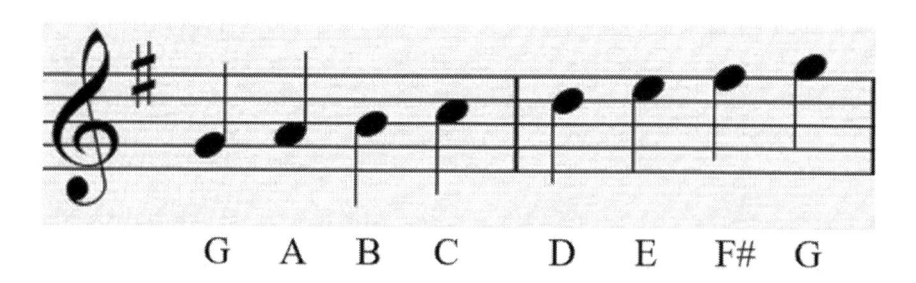

G A B C D E F# G

You can determine the note names in this example by using the same techniques we discussed in the note and rhythm chapter. Use the word FACE to help you find letter names in the spaces,

How to Play Notes on the Saxophone

and EGBDF (Every Good Boy Deserves Fudge) to help you determine letter names of notes on the lines. Remember that we always start from the bottom space or line when using these sayings/phrases.

As mentioned before, each of these notes is played using a different finger placement. The diagram below represents your finger placement on the keys of the saxophone. When a circle is colored black, you will push down that key. If the circle is open, you will leave that key open.

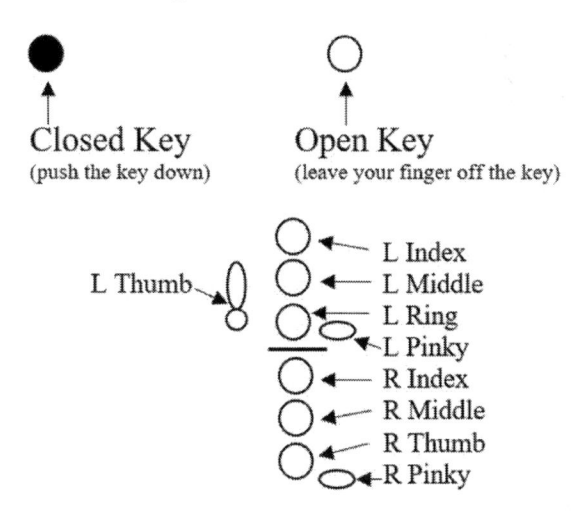

●
↑
Closed Key
(push the key down)

○
↑
Open Key
(leave your finger off the key)

L Thumb

○ ← L Index
○ ← L Middle
○ ← L Ring
○ ← L Pinky
○ ← R Index
○ ← R Middle
○ ← R Thumb
○ ← R Pinky

Let's learn the finger placements for the scale in order, beginning with our G on the second line of the staff.

G Major Scale Fingering Chart

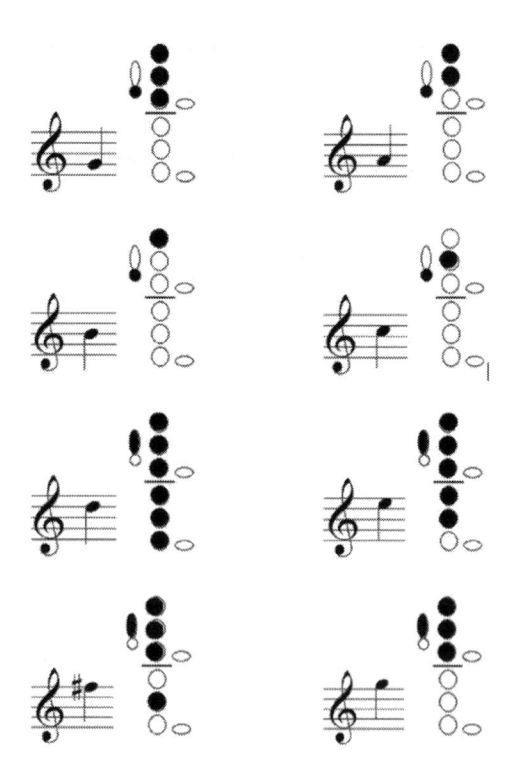

It's important to note that the low G and high G are played using the same finger position, as is true with each note (i.e., low A and high A are also played using the same finger position, etc). There is only one difference in finger position for low notes and high notes of the same letter name: the octave key. If you noticed in the diagrams, the thumb has two separate circles. The bottom, round circle represents the thumb rest, used for all low notes up through C (third space). The top oval represents the octave key. This key is pressed down by the thumb for all notes higher than C in the staff.

> **Listening Example #3: The G Major Scale**
>
> In track 3, listen to the G major scale as it is played in whole notes, half notes, quarter notes and eighth notes. All major scales follow the same pattern, and will sound very similar when played correctly.

Tonguing and Articulation

When you play any note, you will want it to start with a clear, crisp sound (unless otherwise notated in the music). To achieve this, you will want to start each of the notes with your tongue, a technique we call tonguing. Tonguing is a type of **articulation**. Articulation encompasses many techniques that designate the attack, strength, and length of notes.

Once you begin to play notes and music on your saxophone, you will want to get in the habit of tonguing every note. To tongue a note, you will begin by touching the tip of your tongue to the tip of the reed. You can practice how this feels by simply saying "to-to-to-to-to." The placement of your tongue at the beginning of each "to" and its release is an example of the movement your tongue will make while tonguing each note. Next, practice saying "to," but extend the word so it is long and drawn out: "tooooo-tooooo." The T in this word represents tonguing the beginning of each note, and the ooooo represents the air you will use to play this note on your saxophone.

To practice tonguing, start by playing whole notes. Find a note that you feel comfortable playing, and practice starting the note with your tongue each time. You should feel the tip of the reed with your tongue before you play each note, and release your tongue simultaneously as you release your air into the mouthpiece. Once you feel more comfortable with this technique, practice playing half notes and then quarter notes while tonguing each note.

Many beginners mistakenly think they are tonguing the note when they begin the sound using separate bursts of air. This gives them more of a "who" sound that is less clear and defined. You will be able to tell if you are doing this by paying attention to your tongue placement while you play. Does it stay in one spot, or are you moving it from the reed after beginning each note? If your tongue is not moving, you are most likely not tonguing the notes.

Tonguing may feel foreign as you first begin to play your saxophone. It feels unnatural to move your tongue around as if you were speaking while blowing air into your saxophone. Just like any other technique, this will get easier and feel more comfortable with time. Practicing these basic techniques is what will allow you to build a strong foundation and help you play full songs with ease.

How to Play Notes on the Saxophone

> **Listening Example #4:** Tonguing Techniques
>
> In track 4, first listen to notes played on the saxophone *without* tonguing, and then listen to the difference of notes played *with* tonguing. Next, listen to an exercise you can use to practice tonguing with a whole note – half note – quarter note progression.

Chapter 6
Playing Your First Song

Topics Covered:

- Saxophone warm ups

- Scale studies

- Musical examples

You are now ready to start playing some songs on your saxophone! Now that you've learned different notes, rhythms, finger placements, and how to make a sound, let's get to work playing your first song. This chapter will teach you some basic warm ups to play at the beginning of every practice session, more scales to further improve your technical abilities, and a few songs to get started playing.

Saxophone Warm Ups

Warming up is an essential portion of any practice session. Whether you are a beginner or a professional musician, warming up should be the first thing you do each time you play your saxophone. Warming up not only gets air flowing through the instrument, but it allows your fingers and facial muscles to get ready to work hard. Warm ups on wind instruments usually consist of long tones or slow, easy melodies. They also typically involve some scales and technical exercises. While there are no specific exercises you need to play for your warm up, there are a few guidelines you should follow:

- Include some long tones or songs with long notes (such as whole notes)
- Begin with low notes before working your way up to high notes
- Get in the habit of regularly practicing scales

Here are a few examples of potential warm ups you could include in your practice session. Your warm up does not need to take long (just a few minutes) but should always be the first thing you play before diving into your music. Play through each of these exercises at a slow, steady speed to get warmed up before playing your songs. Practice sustaining the sound throughout each measure and do not rush.

Long Tone Exercise #1

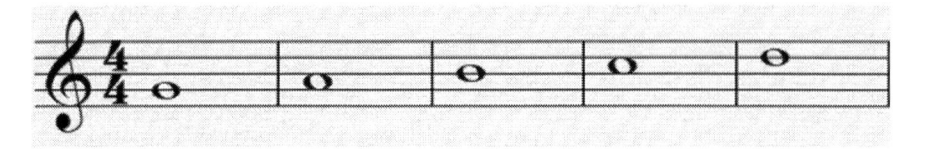

Long Tone Exercise #2

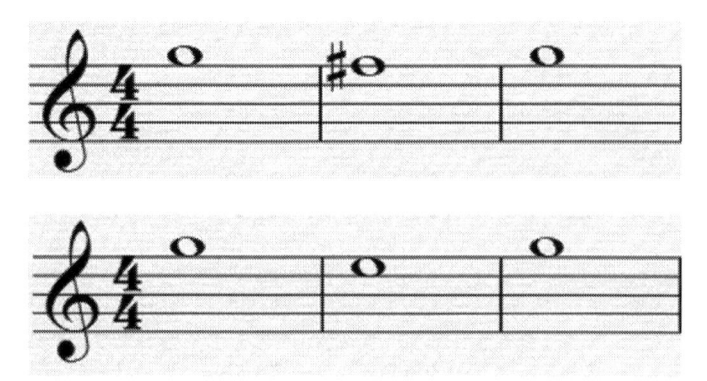

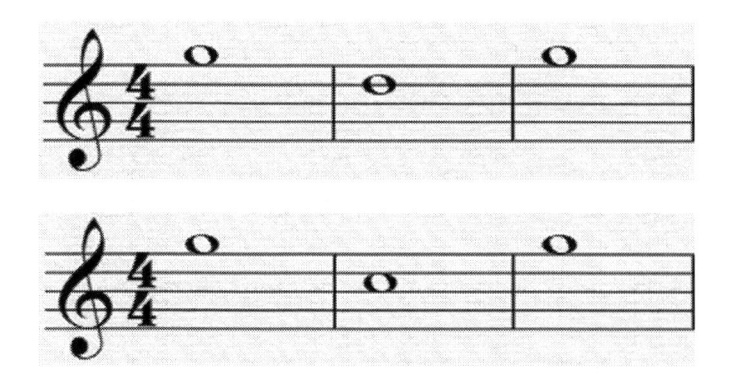

Playing Your First Song

Long Tone Exercise #3

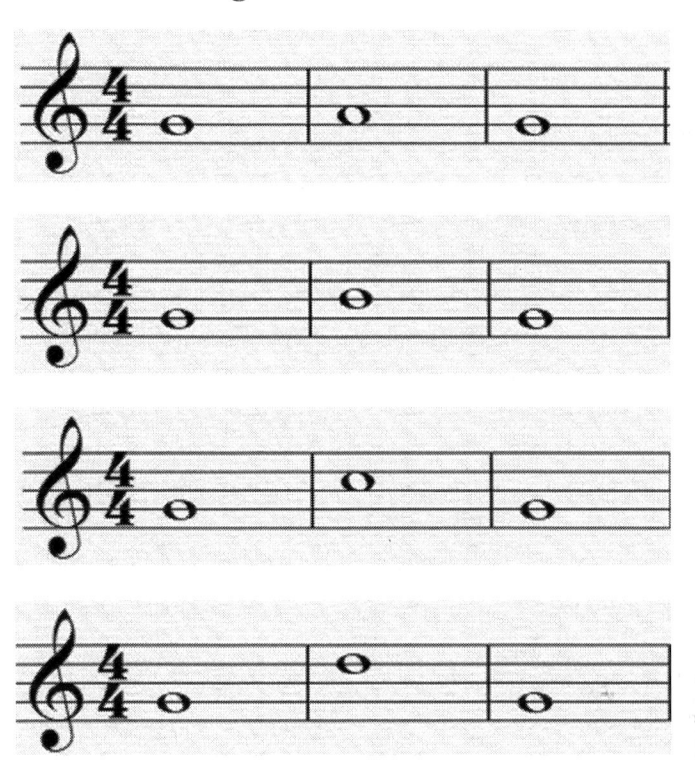

> **Listening Example #5: Long Tone Exercises**
>
> In track 5, listen to long tone exercises 1, 2 and 3.

Scale Studies

Scales are important exercises for any musician. You should get in the habit of regularly playing through one or two scales each time you practice. Scales help you become familiar with different key signatures and combinations of notes, which will eventually improve your site reading and technical skills on the saxophone. Learning the G major scale first (the scale from the previous chapter) is a great place to start.

Once you become familiar with all these notes and can play them with a strong, confident sound, you can begin to learn other scales. The best scales to begin with are the G, D, and C major scales. For your reference, here are all the major scales you can learn on the saxophone:

A Major Scale

D Major Scale

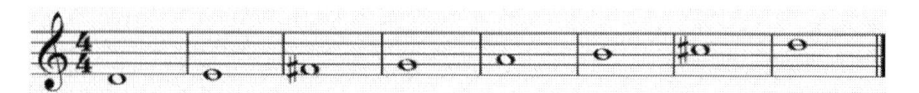

Playing Your First Song

G Major Scale

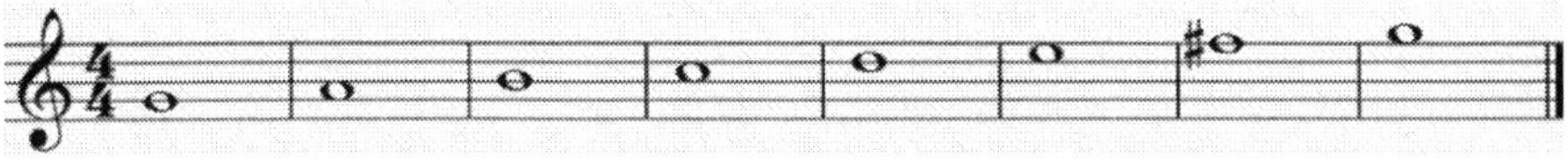

C Major Scale

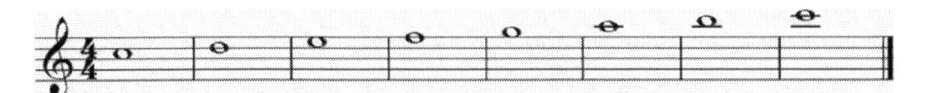

F Major Scale

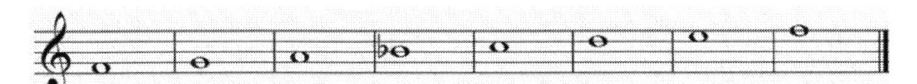

Bb Major Scale

Eb Major Scale

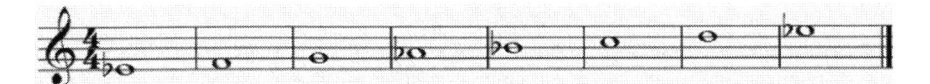

> **Listening Example #6: 7 Major Scales**
>
> In track 6, listen to all 7 major scales played using quarter notes. The scales are played in concert order of the circle of 5ths (the order in which they appear above).

Begin practicing your G major scale each time you play your saxophone. You can play your scale in whole notes, half notes, quarter notes, or any other rhythm you like. Practice going up and then coming back down, starting from the highest note and working your way back down to the lowest note.

It's important to familiarize yourself with one scale before moving on to the next or adding another. All major scales have the same pattern and sound, so practicing one until you can play it confidently will help train your ear to learn the sounds of a major scale. Once you can confidently play the G scale, you can begin learning another – the D major or C major scales are a great next step. Learn your scales thoroughly, one at a time, and practice them with multiple different rhythms each time.

Musical Examples

After spending a few minutes playing long tones and a scale exercise, you are ready to dive into some songs! The possibilities of what you can learn on your saxophone are endless. Beginner saxophone music typically includes just a few notes at one time and the basic rhythms that we learned in the previous chapter. If you come across any notes you do not know, remember to use the saying Every Good Boy Deserves Fudge if the note is on a line and FACE if the note is on a space. I suggest downloading a free saxophone fingering chart that will tell you how to play any note on the saxophone. If you purchased a book of saxophone music, there are often fingering charts in the beginning or on the last page of the book.

It's time to get started playing music! Here are a few songs you can play:

Playing Your First Song

Hot Cross Buns

Listening Example #7: Hot Cross Buns

Twinkle Twinkle Little Star

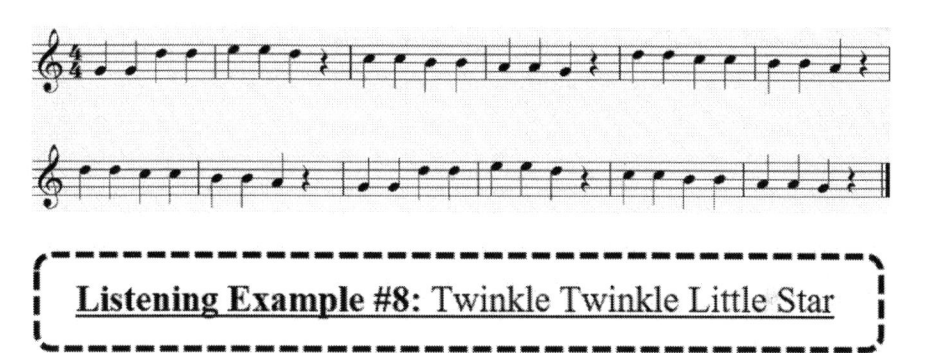

Listening Example #8: Twinkle Twinkle Little Star

Yankee Doodle

There are a few notes in Yankee Doodle that do not appear in the G major scale. For example, the last note in the second measure is below the line. This note is a letter D, and will likely be a note name that you need to memorize, since we cannot use

FACE or Every Good Boy Deserves Fudge to determine its letter name. All of the notes in the second to last measure do not appear in the G major scale either. Luckily, we can use FACE and EGBDF to determine note names for three of them. The first note appears in the bottom space, so using FACE, we can determine that it is a letter F. Since there is a sharp sign in front of it, this note is F#. The third note in this measure appears on the bottom line, so using the saying for EGBDF, we can determine that this note is a letter E.

All the low notes have the same fingering as the high notes, but your thumb will be placed on the circular thumb plate, rather than the octave key. For example, this low F# in Yankee Doodle has the same finger placement as the F# found in your G scale, with the exception of your thumb moving off the octave key.

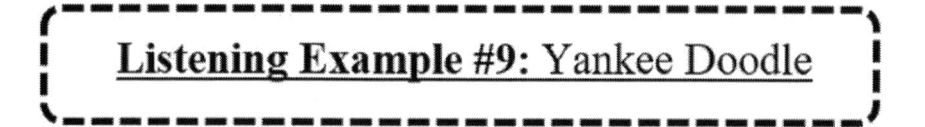

Listening Example #9: Yankee Doodle

Ode to Joy

Listening Example #10: Ode to Joy

Music for many beginner saxophone songs can be downloaded online for free. Check out the resources page at the end of this book for websites from which you can download more songs. These four songs are only the beginning! Once you get started making music on your saxophone, the possibilities are endless.

Chapter 7
Intermediate Saxophone Techniques

Topics Covered:

- Articulation

- Dynamics

- Trills

Now that you've played a few songs on your saxophone and gotten a bit more confident with your sound, it's time to learn a few intermediate techniques. Once you have been practicing for a bit, you may want to learn some more challenging music. When you find more difficult music, there are a few markings and techniques that you will need to know to play it. In this chapter, you will learn more advanced musical notation and a few more advanced techniques to begin practicing on your saxophone.

Articulation

When you first learned to make sounds on the saxophone, you learned about the importance of tonguing. If you remember back from earlier in the book, we discussed that tonguing was a type of articulation. "Articulation encompasses many different techniques that designate the attack, strength, and length of notes." Beginning each of the notes with your tongue separates each note from the next, giving it a clear attack and precise sound.

While you will need to tongue (or "articulate") each note in most songs, there are a few instances where you will *not* tongue the notes. One of them is when you see a **slur**. A slur is a curved marking in your music that appears above or below multiple notes.

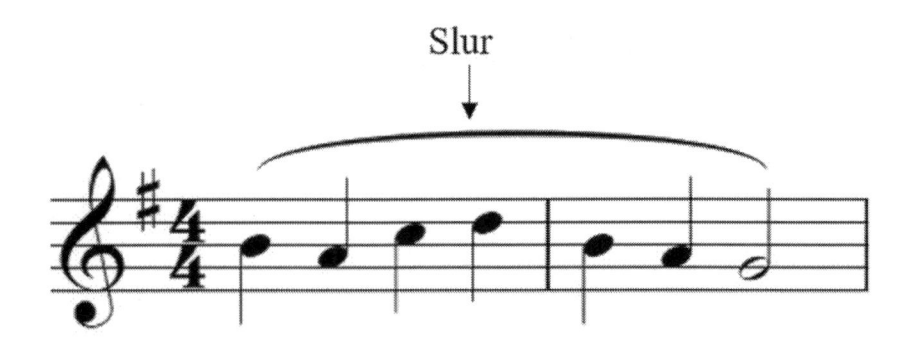

Slur ↓

[musical notation example showing a slur over notes in 4/4 time]

When you see a slur in your music, it means you will not tongue the notes underneath it. You will articulate the first note and continue your air as you move your fingers. Do not stop your air between each note or separate the notes in any way. A slur indicates that this particular section of the music should sound as smooth as possible, with no breaks in the sound for the duration of the slur.

> **Listening Example #11**: Slur Excerpt
>
> In track 11, the exercise above is played first without a slur (tonguing all notes) and then as written, with the slur. Notice the difference between tonguing and slurring.

Intermediate Saxophone Techniques

Another marking that looks like a slur is a **tie**. A tie also appears as a curved marking above or below notes - the difference is that a tie appears above two or more notes that are the same. The tie indicates that only the first note should be articulated and your air should continue without separating the notes. Since the notes are the same, it will sound like one long note. In the example below, you will articulate the beginning of your half note and hold the D all the way through the first beat of the next measure.

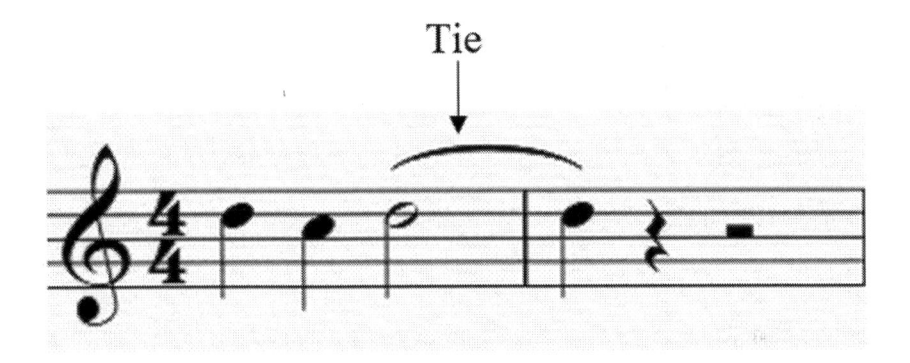

You can differentiate between ties and slurs only by the notes that are underneath the marking. For example:

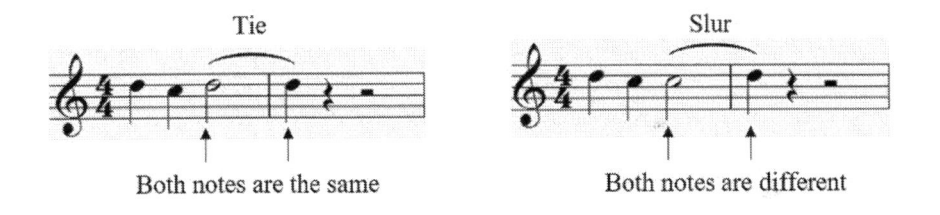

Tie — Both notes are the same

Slur — Both notes are different

Another articulation marking you may find in intermediate saxophone music is a **tenuto**. A tenuto looks like a small horizontal line on top of or below a note. This tenuto indicates that you should play the note smoothly for its full length. When you see a tenuto marking, it designates that the note or notes over which it appears should be played with a legato style.

When you see a tenuto mark, you will still need to tongue the note, but you will do so delicately with a soft attack on the reed. There should still be a definitive start to the note, but little separation and space. Hold the note(s) out for its full length to ensure there is no break or gap in the sound between notes.

As you may notice, the tenuto can appear above or below the note, depending on the direction of the note's stem. When the stem is pointed up, the tenuto will appear below the note, and when the stem points down, the tenuto appears above the note.

In contrast, another articulation marking you may see is a **staccato**. A staccato mark is a small dot that appears above or below a note. The staccato indicates that you should play each note short and separated. Tonguing is very important in sections of music where staccatos appear. You will want each note to sound crisp and clear, with a hard attack against the reed. The note length will be short – just long enough to make a sound and establish a pitch. There should be space heard between each note in a staccato section.

Intermediate Saxophone Techniques

Staccato

One final articulation marking that you may find in intermediate music is an **accent**. Accents are a combination of articulation technique and dynamics. They are most commonly found in marches or other strong, emphasized sections of music. An accent looks like a "greater-than" symbol above or below a note (>). It indicates that the note should be brought out and emphasized. To do so, you will need to play accented notes louder, with a strong attack and space between each note.

Tonging is incredibly important for accented notes; you will need a strong, hard attack against the reed. The beginning of each accented note should be clear and emphasized. Accents are used to bring out a certain note or section in the music. Always remember to maintain a controlled sound when playing accented notes – do not overblow or blow so hard that your tone suffers.

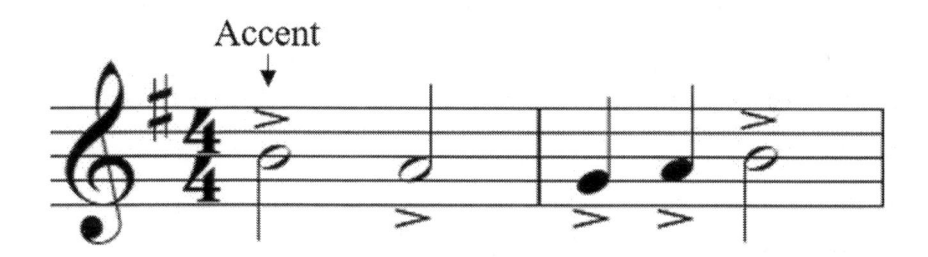

Accent

These five styles of articulation allow you to play a wide variety of music. Adding in different types of articulation really brings a piece of music to life. Using articulation, you can differentiate between multiple sections of the music, give them each meaning, and begin to play with musicality.

> **Listening Example #12:** Tenuto, Staccato, and Accent
>
> In track 12, you will hear the exercise above played three different times.
> The first time, the exercise is played using tenutos.
> The second time, the exercise is played using staccatos.
> And the third time, the exercise is played using accents.

Articulations

- Slur or Tie = Smooth, Connected Notes
- Tenuto = Long Notes, Soft Attack
- Staccato = Short, Crisp Notes
- Accent = Emphasized Notes, Strong Attack

Dynamics

Another musical technique you will find in intermediate saxophone music is dynamics. The word **dynamic** is a musical term that refers to the volume at which the music is performed. There are many types of dynamics, much like articulations. Some dynamics tell you what volume to play an entire section, while others tell you what volume to play a single note. Some dynamic

Intermediate Saxophone Techniques

markings indicate that your volume should gradually increase or decrease. Here are a few dynamic markings to know.

Loud dynamic levels: **forte and mezzo forte**. The most common dynamic markings you will see indicate that a section should be played at either a loud or soft volume. When a section is meant to be played with a strong, confident sound it will be marked with either a forte or mezzo forte. These dynamics are abbreviated *f* and *mf* in music. Forte is an Italian word for loud, meaning that the music should be played at a loud, strong volume.

Mezzo forte is an Italian phrase that means moderately loud. This dynamic level indicates that music should be played with a strong sound, but one step lower than forte. Mezzo forte is often considered to be a normal playing level, whereas forte is the dynamic level where you give it your all. However, forte should never be played in a way that sounds like blasting. Much like accents, remember to never play so loudly that you over blow the note or cause your tone to suffer.

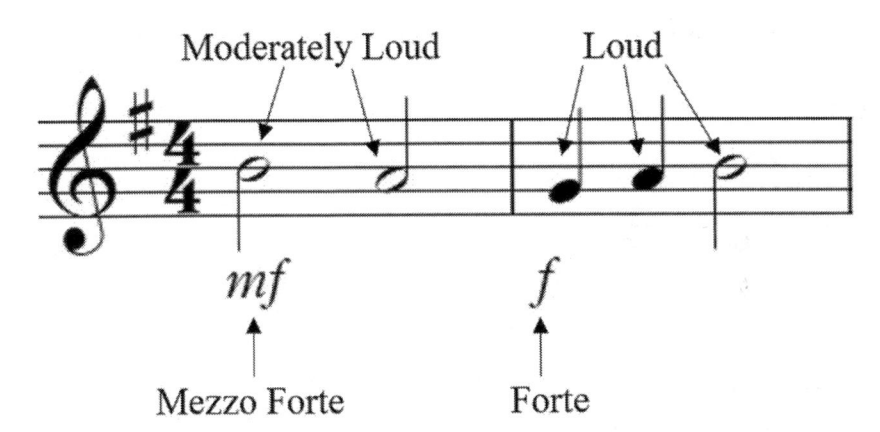

Once a dynamic marking appears in the music, it remains in effect until there is a change. For example, the mezzo forte above would hold true for both the B and A in the first measure, and then would change to forte in measure two until otherwise notated.

Soft dynamic levels: **piano and mezzo piano**. Similar to the previous dynamics, piano and mezzo piano are indicated in music as either *p* or *mp*. Piano is the Italian word for soft. Music at a piano dynamic level should be played quietly. This is the softest dynamic level of the four.

Mezzo piano is the Italian phrase for moderately soft. Music at a mezzo piano dynamic level should be played quietly, but not quite as soft as piano. Mezzo piano is one step louder than piano, but still considered to be a soft volume.

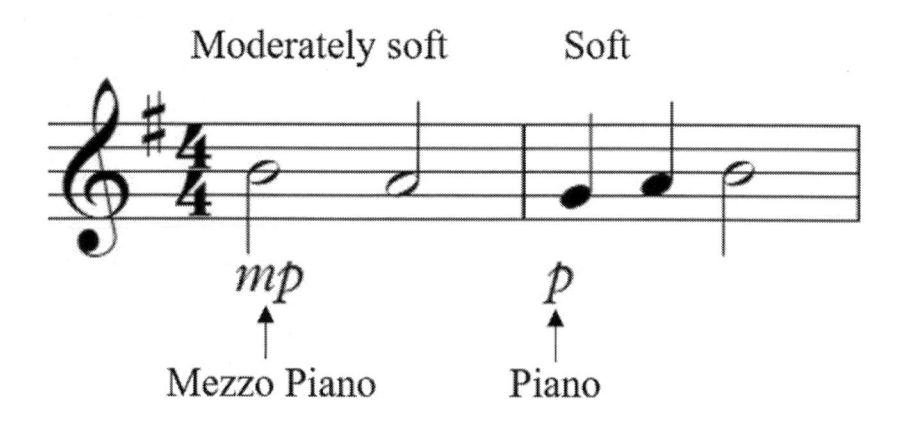

Dynamics can also appear in the form of markings that indicate the music should gradually get louder or softer. The two dynamic markings that indicate this are called **crescendos and decrescendos**. A crescendo or decrescendo can appear for anything from two notes to entire lines of music. A crescendo indicates that you will gradually get louder and a decrescendo indicates that you will gradually get softer. These dynamics typically appear in music as symbols.

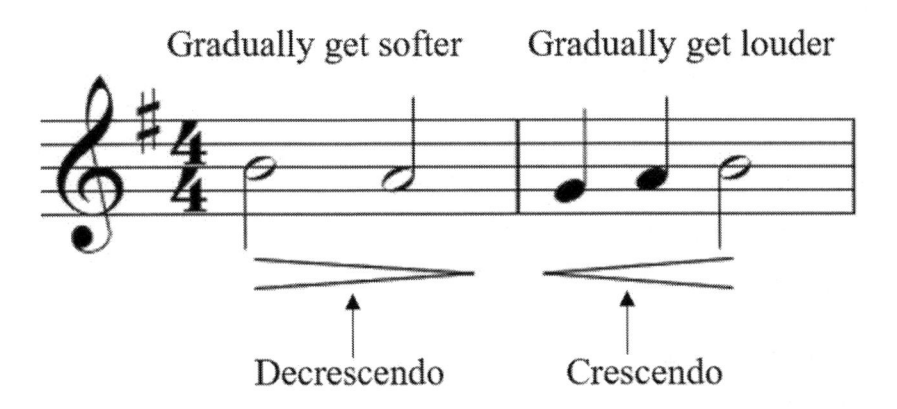

Gradually get softer   **Gradually get louder**

Decrescendo   **Crescendo**

These dynamics always begin with the first note under which they appear. A crescendo means that you will gradually get louder as you play each note that it encompasses. This means that if the crescendo takes place between just three notes, you will need to increase your volume very quickly. If it takes place between three measures of music, you will need to increase volume much more slowly. The same is true for a decrescendo and the rate at which you decrease volume.

> **Listening Example #13: Crescendo and Decrescendo**
>
> In track 13, listen to the example above. Take note of the decrescendo in the first measure, and crescendo in the second. Next, listen to the G major scale played with a crescendo on the way up, and then a decrescendo on the way down.

Crescendo and decrescendo may also be abbreviated as words: *cresc.* or *decresc.* When you see one of these dynamics written in the music in abbreviated form, you can assume that it begins where the word appears and ends at the next dynamic change. This can often mean that a crescendo or decrescendo lasts for multiple measures of music - meaning that you will need to increase or decrease volume very gradually.

Dynamics

- Forte = Loud (*f*)
- Mezzo Forte = Moderately Loud (*mf*)
- Mezzo Piano = Moderately Soft (*mp*)
- Piano = Soft (*p*)
- Crescendo = Gradually Get Louder (<)
- Decrescendo = Gradually Get Softer (>)

Trills

Perhaps one of the most exciting intermediate saxophone techniques is the use of trills. Woodwind music contains frequent trills, especially as you begin to advance in difficulty level. Playing a trill is often fun for beginners.

A **trill** is a rapid alternation between two notes. It is notated in music as "tr~." When you see this notation in your music, it means that you will alternate between the note that is written and one note higher.

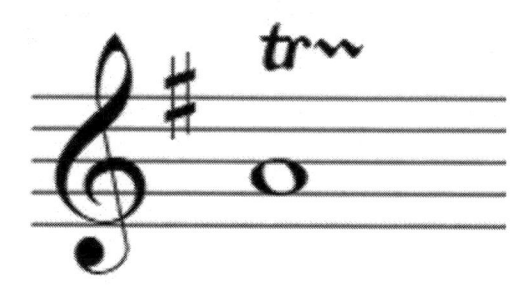

You will always want to slur the notes in your trill, only tonguing the first note (the one that is written), and then rapidly change between the two. Seeing trill notation in your music is the equivalent of playing something like this.

Trills occur rapidly, usually alternating between notes as quickly as possible. If you find that you are unable to change notes quickly due to an awkward finger position, there is probably a trill fingering to aid the transition. A trill fingering is an alternate fingering for the two notes that will allow you to move just one or two keys very quickly. Trilling between two notes in the middle register (the notes that appear on the staff) is often done easily by lifting one finger. For example, trilling between A and B (as seen in the example above) can be done by lifting just one finger.

How To Play The Saxophone

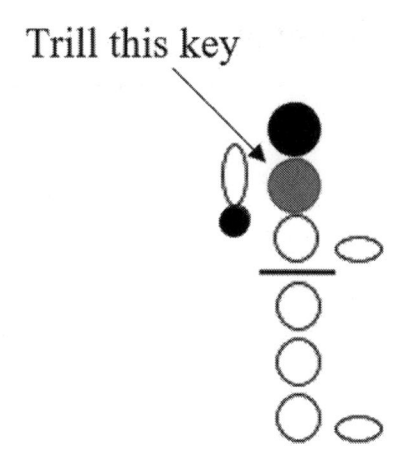

Trill this key

Not all trills will be as easy to complete as this one, so if you find yourself trying to trill between two notes but getting caught up with the finger position, look at a trill fingering chart. You can find most trill fingerings and alternate fingering charts for free online.

> **Listening Example #14: Trills**
>
> In track 14, listen to the G major scale played with a trill on every note. The trill is completed by rapidly alternating between the current note and the note above.

Chapter 8
Conclusion – Bringing it All Together

Learning to play the saxophone is a skill you will use for the rest of your life. Whether you play at home, with your friends, at church, in a jazz group, or professionally – understanding music is a lifelong skill. Making a sound and getting familiar with the notes is the first step. Once you get comfortable reading music and playing notes on your saxophone, the possibilities are endless.

With these techniques and strategies, you will be able to play a wide variety of music. Reading this book was a wonderful first step, and while you will likely know more than most other beginners, there is still so much more to learn. Should you get to a point in your musicianship where you wish to learn more, or are encountering music with notes and techniques outside of what you have learned here, there are a variety of resources you can turn to.

Resources

- Fingering chart
- Tuner
- Saxophone music books
- Saxophone websites

Fingering Chart

It is *highly* recommended that you download or purchase a saxophone fingering chart before you begin playing any music –

whether you need it yet or not. Having a full saxophone fingering chart helps you understand what each key is used for and the differences between all the notes.

If you purchased a saxophone book, there will likely be a full fingering chart in the front or back of the book. If not, there are a variety of websites which allow you to download a fingering chart for free. Here are a couple of places to start:

- https://tamingthesaxophone.com/fingering-chart

- https://www.amromusic.com/saxophone-fingering-chart

- https://www.wfg.woodwind.org/sax/

On your phone, the Fingercharts app is available for free download with Android or Apple. This app allows you to look up specific fingerings, including trill and alternate fingerings.

Tuner Resources

Purchasing or downloading a tuner is a great idea for any musician, regardless of their ability level. Getting in the habit of tuning your saxophone on a regular basis from the beginning will help you establish great intonation and a sense of pitch, and make tuning significantly easier once you get into more advanced literature.

Tuners are available for purchase at any music store. There are a wide variety of options, but all tuners accomplish the same thing. If you decide to purchase a tuner, you may wish to look for one that has a metronome as well. Some more advanced tuners also have an attached microphone, which allows you to tune more accurately if you are in an ensemble setting with multiple people playing.

If you do not wish to purchase a tuner, you can download a variety for free on your phone. There are a great deal of tuner apps; search for them in your app store.

Tuner Apps:

- TE Tuner & Metronome
- insTuner
- Chromatic Tuner

Music Books

Once you feel comfortable making a sound on your saxophone and wish to practice more regularly, purchasing a music book is an excellent choice. There are many beginner saxophone method books that walk you through learning each note, new rhythms, articulations, dynamics, time signatures, and much more. If you are learning on your own without a private teacher, these method books will be a huge help. Some of the most popular method books are:

- Essential Elements
- Accent on Achievement
- Standard of Excellence
- Sound Innovations

If you are studying with a private teacher or in an ensemble, your teacher may have you purchase different etude books or individual solos. A private teacher can help you advance more quickly than you would on your own and select enjoyable music that is challenging, yet attainable.

Websites

There are so many online resources that can inspire you, answer questions, and provide helpful advice, jazz techniques, product reviews, audition tips, and a community. If you are passionate about the saxophone and want to discover more opportunities and inspiration, I suggest finding a community or website to help. Here are just a few of the most popular saxophone websites to get you started:

- https://www.howtoplaysaxophone.org/
- https://tamingthesaxophone.com/
- http://saxhub.com/
- http://www.beginningsax.com/

This is only the start of your musical journey – the possibilities are now endless. Once you begin playing the saxophone you are joining a community of musicians who inspire, challenge, educate, and move others. Enjoy every minute!

If you've enjoyed reading this book, subscribe* to my mailing list for exclusive content and sneak peeks of my future books.

Click the link below:

http://eepurl.com/duJ-yf

OR

Use the QR Code:

(*Must be 13 years or older to subscribe)

Made in the USA
Middletown, DE
13 August 2020